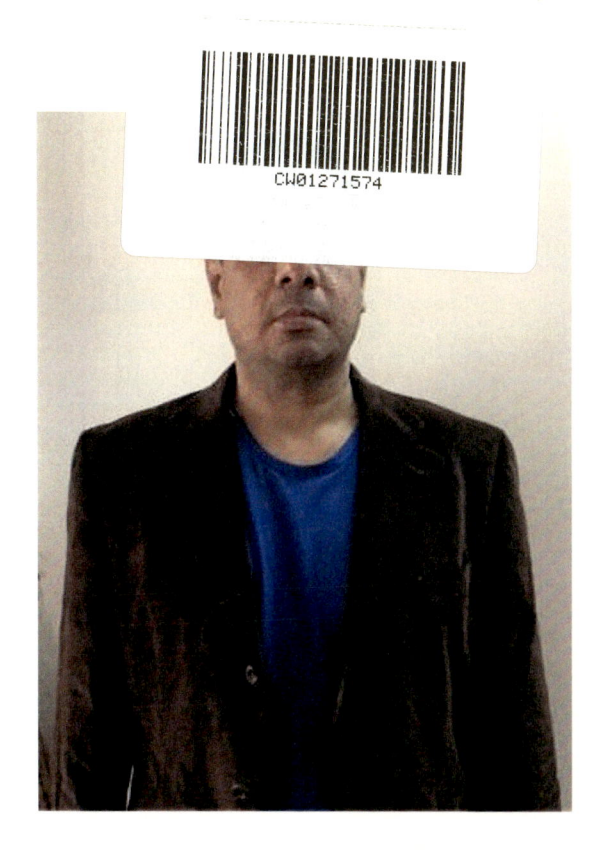

About the Author

Mallikarjun B. Mulimani is a versatile writer. He writes novellas, novels, long and short poems including haikus. His books and style of writing, where brevity is the hallmark, influenced by his engineering background, are unique and highly acclaimed. His writings are crisp, carrying a theme and a message making them highly readable. So far, he has twenty-two books to his credit. They revolve around diverse themes: psychology of humans and their milieu, God, love, sex, religion, realization of self, life and death. They often touch the metaphysical domain.

Death of a Philosopher

Mallikarjun Mulimani

Death of a Philosopher

Olympia Publishers
London

www.olympiapublishers.com
OLYMPIA PAPERBACK EDITION

Copyright © Mallikarjun Mulimani 2022

The right of Mallikarjun Mulimani to be identified as author of this work has been asserted in accordance with sections 77 and 78 of the Copyright, Designs and Patents Act 1988.

All Rights Reserved

No reproduction, copy or transmission of this publication may be made without written permission.
No paragraph of this publication may be reproduced, copied or transmitted save with the written permission of the publisher, or in accordance with the provisions of the Copyright Act 1956 (as amended).

Any person who commits any unauthorised act in relation to this publication may be liable to criminal prosecution and civil claims for damage.

A CIP catalogue record for this title is available from the British Library.

ISBN: 978-1-80074-393-9

First Published in 2022

Olympia Publishers
Tallis House
2 Tallis Street
London
EC4Y 0AB

Printed in Great Britain

Dedication

Dedicated to Reena, The Black Lotus

Acknowledgements

As always, I am indebted to my parents, who have the right to think that they are the creators of the poem below, as I myself am their creation.

Pure

If blue water you stare in is pure
Be sure

You will in it dissolve
And stare at a reflection of above

Encompassing the empty blue sky
Without even a white cloud which at emptiness shouts fie

What then is to say of grey area clouds
In which humankind wallows

Dissolve in emptiness son
That not even the universe will be able to identify your sun

This book could not have been written without the constant encouragement, support, and guidance of Selene, who is in a constant state of endeavour to make me realize the other side of the coin:

Selene

What keeps me energized every morning
Are your messages which keep me striving

For that God you believe in
And in whom I don't have trust in

What kind of a paradox am I stuck in?
Can I be released from my within?

Author's Note

> In the red
> I bled
> To nightmares forget
> And youthful dreams resurrect

Death of a Philosopher, *DOAP*, began as an exercise in a different domain of creativity. After writing twenty-two books, I was tired of writing, and with passing age, I began to look back fondly towards my childhood days where I absolutely loved sketching and painting. One fine day, I decided to be an exuberant kid again, and rediscover the creativity associated with pictures, but alas, my hand could not sketch or paint any more; however, during my engineering days, I had dabbled with quite some measure of success in Computer Art, and that period of time obviously being closer to my present, I decided to pick up Computer Art once more. So, using Paint, available in Microsoft Windows, and images freely available on the Internet, I began creating comic strips, which portrayed my philosophy with a brevity which surpassed its predecessors in the books I had written till then, and created around one hundred and sixty of them; however, there were no takers for my new art. I was tired, and decided to take a break from my creativity. I found myself in Goa, completely relaxing, and then, as creativity would have it, my love for writing came rushing back to me on the crests of waves kissing the beach. I began to write *DOAP* right there and then, drawing from the Computer Art I had created at home, and continued writing long after I came back.

On a different note, this is my twenty-third book, and the reason for me picking up a discarded manuscript of mine, and completing it, can hopefully be found in *DOAP's* Epilogue. Many questions about my lifetime's work will be answered after my twenty-fourth and twenty-fifth books are published.

I have used the word, 'Creativity', many times, so, what exactly is creativity according to me? Creativity is no one thing, and nothing else in this universe is just one thing too. Creativity, as understood by me, can be:

Creativity is the blossom blooming on the tree of effort in spring. The blossom, creativity, is not permanent, does not last after spring, but the tree, effort, should remain almost constant, relaxing only in spring, so that the blossom, blossom without any more effort. Constancy, as in every other sphere of life, including life itself, is impossible in creativity. It is the age-old principle of 'Hold fast and let go', which works miracles for creativity, as it does for everything else in life.

Everything is contained within us, for ultimately, there is no true objectivity, but only subjectivity, and creativity too is contained entirely within us. Superconsciousness is not external, but internal. It is our unconscious, subconscious, and consciousness working together in sync. It is this superconsciousness that we should tap into to find true creativity, which bursts in bursts.

Creativity is not even being yourself.

But, since an external superconsciousness obviously does not exist, creativity does not flow from it through a hollow bamboo and reach your consciousness.

Creativity is what you free yourself from and it comes into

being.

You are not creativity and neither is creativity you. It just exists in the multiverse free from those who strive for it.

Stop trying to be creative, and you are, but, mark it, it is never yours, as nothing else in the multiverse is. Open the palm of your hand, and the whimsical butterfly of creativity alights to mesmerize you.

Be in love, and that is the greatest creativity, for nothing can capture or define it.

You are either in love or you aren't.

Preface

It was difficult to write a Preface for this book as it is but a collection of staccato bursts of philosophy; however, I have tried, as it has become a habit of mine nowadays to use brief, symmetrical, and rhyming poems, whenever possible, to convey my message, to write this Preface using poems.

What Happy felt throughout DOAP:

Life Again, Damn

Life being
What am I living
At myself staring

If but I could
Understand myself as I should
Life lived be would

If in a mirror
I stare at another
Who is me, brother

Lies discarded
Truths amalgamated
Born is eternity discarded

For in this moment
With my complementary parent
My life is well spent

Winner

When you stare
At death in its face bare

It averts its gaze
And you are out of the maze

In which life put you in the first place
And you will have found your place

No more will you have to apologize
For mistakes which cut others down to size

Why worry
When others lowly have to be sorry

You are free
Don't you see

None can control you
Be you

For it is your life
Be without strife

Love

If love
Is my dove

Above
What others consider above

Their stupidity in stow
And in nonsense below

I with you my love
Will fly over heavens above

The last two poems of Happy, after he had happily settled on the mainland, which he wrote sitting by a pristine blue lake surrounded by lush green mango trees bearing vibrant yellow mangoes:

Lake Kelgeri

On these banks
Containing joy beyond World Banks

Youth to me is returned best
With added interest

Here springs poetry
Which needs no chemical entry

I am finally free
To be

Mango Tree

King of fruits
King of solitude

Gather
Together

Koels coo
For me too

And I realize
In the summer fragrance

That life is beautiful
And I am too

Men, if they think without women, aren't

To find commonality in the common is not uncommon, but to find a blood diamond seeks even the blood of the diamond

Happy

Happy sat unhappy.

He thought: a very dangerous thing.

He was on the seashore and he was thinking: stupid!

Happy was a stupid mental laborer, whose life, like that of physicals', depended almost entirely upon his own efforts. If one day he would get to have a physical chat with his online intellectual friend Selene, he would say, "Peace is but best not spoken!".

Once Selene, the poetess, drifted into Happy's mind, he immediately wrote a poem right on the beach where he was, simply because:

> The young man and the sea
> Were the butterfly and the bee
> The graceful flight of the boy
> The stinging spray of the sea shouting ahoy
>
> But it would come to be
> That the young man would return to normal life
> For in the ordinary
> Lies the extraordinary
>
> One can't while away one's life
> Whatever may be the cause of strife
> Poems are best written on the beach

> But life elsewhere also has much to teach

In a flash, Happy's suddenly unencumbered mind, remembered that it was his mother's birthday that day. Beautiful women are together!

He softly wrote another poem on the beach that was turning pleasantly hot:

> Leaves home woman fiery
> Like waves at the beach
>
> Crying in her finery
> To the horizon I go to motherhood preach
>
> But alas, horizon is an unreachable destination
> Where only in-laws screech
>
> Soon children too escape in teenage confusion
> But aged husband provides consolation
>
> During life's sunset mother attains realisation
> That in the boat of husband and wife had lain the sun
>
> That her hubby had always been the one
> Who was the catch of every season

Happy came back to his mess as flagrantly as he had left.
'Why have I come here?
'Why is it such an undefinable?
'How have I come here?
'Simple...

'Because I have money, my father's.
'And that is the death of a philosopher.'
Surf was pounding. His mind was throbbing.
Waves were crashing. His mind was breaking.
Like relentless waves, thoughts swept over him.
'Life is a trauma, to be survived and died.
'Cancer of the soul; when such a thing doesn't exist!
'Why do we live the way we live and how we live?
'Because we do not know how to do what to.
'Life is simple, so what is the death of a philosopher?
The death of a philosopher is his life.'
What was Happy's unhappy life all about?
What was life all about?
Lost love.
Was it worth it?
Not even time can tell.
Sex?
Obviously, for without it, humanity would be dead.
So why did he do it?
So that time could tell…
Will he be happy?
Or will he drown in the sea of misery?
Night fell.
Life was flies on his computer screen; itching on his legs. Black sea in front of him; black like the future of humanity!
He thought again:
'Who is to decide what? Not God!
'Who is God? Your savior! Your timekeeper!
'But then what is time? Time is but a series of convoluted events thought and unthought! So why bother?
'Life is just insecure, so you better be secure.'

There was a beautiful brown woman beside the brown Happy; he had asked for a friend, and she was sizing him up.

He knew that it was no mistake; he was just one gentleman among lecherous men ogling her. So, actually, he was not a gentleman, but only a male looking for a convoluted version of the desire to procreate with a condom.

She left him after sizing him up; his desire for truth had spoken volumes about his unspoken lie.

Confusing, yes. The truth is that there is no truth.

She had come and gone on the barstool beside him many times. He was a fool who refused to bend, and was left alone at night.

Nights are great if you don't sleep and are at peace, but what is peace?

Morning finds him writing to his friend whom he will never meet; for disappointments abound in person in the universe.

Life is words; that has made man, man.

The sea is inviting Happy. He is still unhappy, and writes a melancholic poem:

To be free of desire requires desire. To recognize this greatness requires greatness. And who this accepts, life accepts

He adds prose to poetry:

"Life is... Please input dear friend Selene."

She has understood him like no other. She is his alter ego; twin.

"Life is lust.

"Lust for life; lust for death.

"Whether you live or die is up to you!

"Why am I writing what I am writing?

"Definitely not for you and also not for me....

"For who am I? Another consciousness...

"And what is consciousness but an accident of nature!
"And I am in nature…
"So why am I writing?
"To understand?
"No.
"I am beyond that.
"Probably trying to tell people that there is nothing to understand.
"Nothing, excepting maybe love…
"But can it be understood?
"If it could have been understood, then there would have been no dearth of love.
"And the universe would have been happy. I am the unhappy Happy!
"My story is the story of Happy, who wanted to be happy, like everybody else, and failed, like everybody else.
"For happiness is not a destination, it is the source."

Selene replied that she loved his last sentence. She was happy. Happy wished he could be happy like Selene.

He sat on the seashore wondering why all are unhappy. He knew that the search for happiness was the cause of unhappiness, but he was human, and one can't be anything other than human. Humanity's other name is suffering. No man is a Buddha, not even the Buddha himself. Lust drives men and women to shores unreachable. They become castaways of their own making. But there is no helping this condition. Slaves on ships of desire all are. Rowing away for bastard masters. Happy knew all are masochists; for, without pain there is no pleasure, and all want pleasure, so they are entitled to pain. Without this yin and yang, life is death, and nobody wants to die.

Twilight…

'What is beauty?' thought Happy.

He was unhappy because he knew that beauty couldn't be defined; like God! And men waste their entire lives in searching the unsearchable. But men don't stop, do they? And neither do the indefatigable women! And therein lies misery; in the search!

Beauty is beauty; no thought!

If you try and open a wine bottle, you screw and get screwed. Simple.

We are influenced by even the tiniest flutter of a butterfly's wings.

Why do we think we are in control?

Happy started becoming happy.

Selene had messaged him.

But she was his exact opposite; she was happy.

She was happy because she believed in the impossible; and Happy didn't know what was possible; he was lost; as all men are. Women, like the moon, are contented. They are satisfied with the earth. They are mother earth.

Happy was unhappy because he was on mother earth and wanted the sun. He loved the unreachable moon. He was confused.

Selene was unreachable because she was the moon, and he did not like the earth. To take off, you need a launch pad.

Impossible things, like God, are impossible.

Selene believed in the impossible.

Repressed is eternity suppressed.

That afternoon, Happy had met a person who had committed a half-murder; a person from a neighbor country like his once friend who too had been exiled to Happy's country.

Happy had been happy to meet the almost killer. That fellow had not been repressed; Happy had become less depressed. For to try and kill is the will of almost all. We kill ourselves almost daily for almost no reason. This chap had just tried to avenge the insult of his sister. Happy had told the genuine guy, "Aren't we all sons of our mothers, and brothers of sisters?"

The happy fellow had told Happy, "You are cool!"

Happy had also met two lawyers who were not at all repressed. They had agreed that there is no right or wrong, but only blind law.

As night fell, Happy was becoming happy, for he could deduce that there is no philosophy in life! But only life! Love of wisdom is no wisdom. Death of a philosopher was progressing beyond death.

Happy decided to have one more scotch. He then decided that life is a lemon and redecided to have lemonade instead. Happy's father would become happy at his son's decision. He then called up his father.

Happy died that night. He had imbibed values from two great religions radically opposed to each other and at opposite ends of a three-dimensional spectrum that had in its middle another which had educated him; but his parents were from another that was supposed to teach tolerance. He was tolerant and had smoked great pot from a bong. He had smoked it with a beautiful lady, who loved David, and who, with each drag, had told him, "Bless You". A great guy, whom Happy deeply loved, and who was from the latest of the three religions, had stopped meeting him. You see, both the lady's and the guy's loved ones had died in rival bomb blasts.

The guy did not care a damn about religion, but the lady did, so Happy had learnt that tolerance comes in various forms. The guy had tolerated Happy mingling with someone who he knew would not like him, and therefore, had kept his distance. The lady had educated Happy about God, and Happy had become happy. Life is God and sex, nothing else. The guy and Happy had talked of nothing but getting some, and they had gotten some. Grass came with God into the picture with the lady, and there is no difference among the three intoxicants. The lady had told Happy, not asked, "Can you, with your philosophy and science, give meaning to life? Why are we here? What accounts for this diversity in nature? We are sitting beside the sea, the smallest in it lives with the biggest, and on land, the lion with the lamb!" She had intoxicated and befuddled Happy. She had calmly, laughingly, and beautifully, dismantled him.

But Happy had not become sad, but incredibly happy. But he had not met the guy again. That night, Happy slept and died. When his heart stopped long after midnight in the heat of his shack, and his mind was being wrenched away into a deeper darkness like hell, and not into light due to his mortal sins, when every nanosecond — nanoseconds could be agonizingly felt — Happy heard his soul praying, "Let me live God!" And there was life. This is fate, if nothing else.

Happy, the atheist philosopher, had died, and was born an agnostic. We live and die so many times in life. That is the Buddha's rebirth. Happy woke up early, both happy and sad, had lemonade, orange juice, cheese and toast, and rose to scotch by early morning. The "Bless you" lady did not meet him that next day, as she had promised, but she had given him her number, and her email address. Happy messaged her, sent her his book about Yin & Yang philosophy, which both had vehemently agreed upon, and would soon leave the shack beside the sea. Sometimes, a religious fanatic teaches one more than a nonreligious comrade! This was another death of a philosopher. What we think is, never is. What we want, we get.

Happy had spent many days in his shack beside a bar on the beach and had had numerous escapades. The false infinity was his true goal.

An Ethiopian lady had taught Happy about love, but, even though she was the most beautiful woman he had ever been with — only the second — Happy had talked the softness out of her with his unnecessary philosophy. He was impotent because of his love for love and scotch. Happy decided he would go home happy. Also, that he would play around with a lot of heads on his way back; for even though he would have become physically weak, he would have become mentally invincible. *'This is to be my happiness,'* thought Happy.

Happy learnt something by the sea. He learnt that when one stops talking, one can listen to the sea, others, and most importantly, oneself. But that was not to be the end of his misery regarding words. He understood that words have this insane ability to divide. He realized the futility of holy books. He decided to act. In the morning, he started cleaning the table he had sat at the previous day. He struggled, but succeeded! The stewards he had called his friends became his brothers. Actions speak louder than words. Happy finally understood this and the futility of his verbose philosophy. He rejected all holy books and his books too. He realized that if one just listened, without straining the tongue in the least bit, one could come to know and love a lot. Everybody suffers, and they want a kind ear, and a hug does more wonders than a split tongue. Vasudeva had taught Siddhartha how to listen, to the water of the river. The Ethiopian lady had talked a lot about water. Happy had understood Siddhartha's Kamala a little. Everybody wants something: God, sex, which is love in convoluted forms, so as to survive and procreate, an escape, just like how drugs facilitate an escape… But a kiss by Kamala had done wonders for Siddhartha, and it had worked for Happy too. He had learnt from Vasudeva and Kamala, the black lotus. He was Siddhartha. He wanted nothing and had everything. But would it last without money? The ultimate intoxicant!

The "Bless you" beautiful white lady had told Happy, "I don't understand why you like your once colonizers so much! What must your countrymen and women think of you?" She had added vehemently but in her very own charming manner, "I and all of my people detest the very same once colonizers of yours for they had colonized my country too. They tried to destroy us." Happy didn't know much history, and the darling lady was his virtual schoolmate, as both believed in living in the moment, but she had seemed to be certain of such matters, and Happy of others.

He had smiled his wan smile and added wistfully, "What are we without communication? We are conversing because of our once colonizers who granted us their language, else wouldn't I have missed your charming company and delightful words? Why shouldn't we be grateful for what the ungrateful forcefully yet gracefully bestow upon us?" She had smiled and, upon immediately receiving a call, started talking in her mother tongue. She had later showed her messages to Happy, and Happy had understood that these chosen proud men and women chose their native language over those of his and her nations' once colonizers, while he — an unchosen yet immensely proud man, a writer, poet, and philosopher — as he had so got embellished on his visiting cards, loved the universal language of his once colonizers, and it was very rare that he talked or even thought in his nations or mother tongue. He was trying maintain a stiff upper lip, always, though more than once, he gave into the hot blood of his tropics. Happy, the writer, loved language, and Happy, the philosopher, hated language. To talk or not to talk was the conundrum, and meanwhile, poetry was a matter of the heart and not the brain.

If Happy really looked inside himself, he would just find a poet minus the writer and the philosopher, unencumbered by laws and conventions, but, fortunately or unfortunately, Happy was living in a society, and what are we without our relationships, good and bad? But, then again, when an artist, a poet, is unencumbered by societal norms, he is bound to be more vicious, in all forms of expression, wild… Inside, Happy had been Emile Zola's 'The Human Beast', tortured by 'Lust for Life' like Irving Stone's Van Gogh, lust for love and sex, something without which no man or woman is complete, trying to find meaning in the books of evolution by Darwin and Dawkins. But now, here in paradise, his inside had become the outside, and hence, all was one. Happy had cast off society's garments and become his own and Desmond Morris's 'The Naked Ape'.

Happy had met a black girl, a white, and a brown. He couldn't decide which one of them was more beautiful, even though he was brown and the brown girl had unabashedly allowed him to click gorgeous photographs of her! Happy had talked about water with the black and about Yin & Yang with the white. He had written a book, 'Rivers', and another, 'Predator & Prey', which was based upon Yin & Yang! The black was the birth of humanity and the black and white its essence. The lady of the chosen tribe had waxed eloquent about the Yin & Yang intrinsic to life. The Ethiopian had flowed smoothly like water with him. Both were the pinnacle of his stay in paradise. The browns were a mere shadow, a grey area, absolutely necessary to deal with practical life, but not with passionate life! The Ethiopian was a quiet one and the chosen one a vivacious one. The latter had made it clear that white is absent without black. Happy had quietly agreed. He had not said much, as he didn't have to, after all he had written an entire damned book on the holy topic. The lady had said, "Bless You!"

Happy had been unhappy without the company of delightful ladies for long, and now he was tremendously happy without being suffocated by his own happiness. He was loved by all on the beach. They liked him for he did not intrude. He intruded only with his own ideas, which were neither borrowed nor packed with talk of unnecessary people. There are both necessary and unnecessary people: necessary people who share ideas of their own and the unnecessary ones who impart ideas about necessary people. Happy and the ladies were above the unnecessary. They stayed only with what was necessary, and for all people, the necessary is money. All of them agreed upon that.

Happy had understood that agony began where you do not accept yourself for what you are and instead want others to like you; the more the better; and the more the number of former friends and girlfriends or boyfriends, the much better! One doesn't let go, for if one does, one's past is lost, and hence, one's present and future too. Happy wanted to prove the unnecessary philosophy of letting go wrong, but couldn't. Everyone had kept their eyes on him, and his own follies with his own devices and tongue hadn't helped. Nobody accompanies you into death, and Happy had died innumerable times during his life, and he had written this crap in his books, but no more! Life should be all and only about life. Happy decided to live life, free from all former girlfriends, the one who had almost completely accepted him and those who had not because he had not tried hard enough because of the one permanently impermanent in his life. Chaotic life would soon be brought to order by Happy's life itself. He thought, *'Partaking from Rumi, life sets itself into order; but only if you let it, flow with it, stop imposing your damned ideologies upon it, but primarily, upon yourself. Free yourself from your very own philosophies, simply live, let it be the death of a philosopher, and the birth of a lover, of all and everything in life! People don't understand that you are so much old only once, and that the sand grains in life's hourglass are constantly dropping into the grave.'* The sea swooshed onto the beach. "I will love," said Happy, but to no one in particular, at sunset, for the gorgeous white lady was trying to define the sunset, and he was trying to undefine both them and himself, so that he could be one with all beauty. Happy had understood. *'Even a poet cannot define a sunset, but even if the poet can, he or she shouldn't try, if he or she really wants to be happy,'* thought Happy, angry with the word, "enjoy", used frequently by other people on the beach. *'There is no "en" in "joy", it is supposed to be the internal joy of solitude,'* happily internalized Happy.

Happy understood something which seemed to him profound, 'That struggle is peace, that peace is success, and that success comes in various forms, and one of the forms is that very struggle for peace.' Happy was happy because he was constantly struggling.

The writer and philosopher Happy had understood something else simultaneously, 'That no matter how good a writer and philosopher one is, one cannot help a caterpillar enjoy scotch until it is ready. You can only guide some, and that too only some of the way, till they decide to take a drink of the holy water, but it is up to them to become intoxicated! That most caterpillars do not become butterflies at all, but remain worms, and even most who do grow to sprout wings, become dark moths unable to experience the spirit of the day.' Happy was a butterfly.

The brown lady had asked Happy how much he could spend in an hour on his drink alone. Happy had gladly given her four times the amount for two hours, for you see, Happy liked to talk. But, then again, Happy also liked to drink a lot, so he was almost broke for the day when he broke off with the lady, mentally satisfied. Happy was called an unhappy fool by his comrades on the beach, but from inside, he was happy, and nobody could take that away from him.

'What are women?' thought Happy, *'Mind or matter?'* *'Both,'* he decided, *'for life is Yin & Yang, and what are we men but dice rolled by women,'* and fell laughing, but not off his perch upon a barstool, for his mind was unfortunately still stable. Unhinged men are the best, for they go to their deathbeds untested. It is only the sane who suffer.

Happy suddenly understood the fact of the universe, the birth, the non-essence of individual men, for it can be any man, but that the mother is one, that she is the only one, the mother of all irresponsible men. Happy felt stupid. Why had he been running after one woman and not a mother? That was why he was alone… Happy felt sad. Happy felt sad at his stupidity. But life does not care for either Happy's happy, sad, or stupidity. The mother nature moves on with her ridiculousness…

Happy cried ridiculously but seriously after he thought of all women as those of the world's oldest profession. Happy cried profusely as he thought of the only woman he had loved and had tried to forget with other women. He could not. He could not for he was a lover, but she was not, and that had led to the death of a philosopher. Happy was stuck in shit. His philosophy could not help him, and Selene, his intellectual friend, had taken a home leave. All have homes, but Happy had never felt at home anywhere. This was his misfortune. Happy was a wanderer, a traveler through desperate fields of gold trying to woo their God! But Happy was amalgamated out of disturbed sand. Happy became unhappy with his philosophy. He couldn't cry out to the sky, "Help me God!" as he had once done, for he had once and once more become undone.

After being dismantled by lovers, friends, and family, Happy stood like the straight areca palm tree that rose tall in front of him in his buddy's home, advertising its intoxication to the Heavens when he was about to take leave of his second mother to go to his enlightenment in another home. Existentialism had seemed real to him, then and now. A needle reaching into the sky and earth, all alone, and stupendously smooth, shiny, and wonderfully sleek!

Happy was an unsuccessful writer because he was a philosopher. Nobody liked his philosophy of not using names of persons in his evolving books. Unfortunately, he also believed that one has to have lived the tale one is telling to at least half its extent. His life was pure Yin & Yang and nobody could relate to that as all thought of themselves as pure Yang. His friends, relatives, and family were constantly stabbing him in the back, for they were all men and women of a particular caste, religion, and creed, and he was of none except the one of the universes. However, Happy's philosophy of Yin & Yang used to become dismantled when he admired the third sex, the best of both worlds. He had been chided by the editor of his defining book when he had talked about only two sexes in the universe, but he had stuck to his guns and argued that the ordinary will not like me talking about the extraordinary. The lady editor had agreed, and only two sexes came to be in the book. Happy had loved it when the Ethiopian lady had also expressed interest in his interest in the third sex. After all, Happy had got the name 'Bucephalus' painted in black on his white car and his password was 'Achilles'. Happy was in the company of great men like Alexander and Achilles. But they were dead, and he soon would be too one fine day. But he wished to become immortal like them; with their love for war and love! Happy waged war on society. He exposed to all every strength of his which they loved to call as weaknesses. Happy became stronger. He was becoming the 'Invictus' of William!

Happy had once invented an analogy to the Myth of Sisyphus with his imaginary lover. Both had said that, "No matter how many times men keep measuring, theirs will remain small." Happy had then drifted off into greener pastures, "The only solution of life is penetration, primarily into the organic and then into the inorganic. All else is false. Life is from chaos to chaos, so don't struggle. Life is capable of many things. It is capable of imagining God!"

Happy became sad at his train of thoughts, and sought peace in the thought, *'Peace is not keeping the mind empty, but filling it with the right stuff.'*

Peace was to Happy what freshwater was to a castaway on a paradise island in the sea. One can write any number of books, but until one earns money from them, accolades by aristocrats feed only one's ego and not the soul. He spent money he had but hadn't earned, and that ruined the peace he was always seeking to buy. He was a shark among intellectual dolphins, a survivor who sought death through hedonism because there was dearth of the right company in his life. Happy had come to the seashore paradise trying to love the money which made it possible to find love with money, for he knew an open secret which most holy men abhorred, that it is in actual physical contact that loneliness can be forgotten, a new connection made with a complementary body. Happy had said this vehemently to all the three ladies, separated by time and space, "Holy men clandestinely kiss other cheeks because they want exactly what the unholy men want!" Happy had found a soft warm hand upon his knee, like in 'Another Harry's Bar' by Jethro Tull, on one of these instances. He had then become unhappy, "How much money can do is tremendous, how much it can belittle is too," for he himself sometimes became small in the mirror, however, another instance of belittling was, no matter how small he actually became, others with maya glasses in front of their eyes used to keep on worshipping him as the magnificent David. The white lady had talked about the lust of men, kings, David himself, and Happy, when he had started hearing a familiar story in which the handsome king had acquired the bathing wife of one of his subordinates, had immediately piped up, 'Bathsheba'! The lady, who had previously only genuinely smiled at his mispronunciation of the names of her chosen people, had corrected him this time, but gently. Happy had again felt greatly indebted to and proud of his father who lay ailing and waiting back home like the wise Solomon. His father had made him all that he was, an impregnable writer, impregnable by his readers themselves, no penetration, probably, his father had wanted his son to remain straight! Happy had said in a rush to the gorgeous white lady with brilliant black curls like those on his brown energetic head, "All writers born write the same stuff, trying to understand life till the end of their lives, but one has to understand Shoonya, that the beginning and the end are one and the same." She had not understood, and filling her bong with water, and mediocre native grass, lighted it with a huge lighter she had procured in her new home. Happy, becoming desirous of such knowledge, which scotch alone cannot give, had gently begged the bong out of her hand and teased it to his mouth. The lady was such a gentlewoman, that later, she had herself wiped Happy's probable virus stains off the mouth of the bong. Happy, though, slightly zonked, had said, "Good bong, but we come from the primordial soup of Darwin and Dawkins, and into the ecosystem we go." Happy was liberated and hence he could say such things and she could refute such things, but, where would both, and the rest of the world be, when sober?

As both had parted, long after midnight, there had been loving words, by both:

"Don't try to fill your life, let it be filled, by itself."

"Life is the problem of and solution to itself; just live!"

Nobody in the annihilated bar had been able to distinguish between the words of the two!

Happy had been left happily exhausted at this stage:

There's no anger, there's no hate, but only colour which screams my fate. Will I make it a rainbow, or a shroud to date, depends upon many a light which I choose to light

Happy's unhappy problem was that he was unhappy in love. What is love? Love was not an illusion for Happy. It was tangible, throbbing, in the form of his pulsating lover who had deserted him. Happy was screwed up and trying to screw simply because life had screwed him up with her as its accomplice. So where was the justice in all this? The French professor, in front of whose home he had seen existentialism in a tree which bred intoxicants, had told him that there was God, but she did not believe justice had been done to her, and that Happy should get married and settle down! *'What an absurd amalgamation of insanities,'* thought Happy, though his soul, which he knew didn't exist, screamed for God and Justice and shit! Life was a screwed-up corkscrew for Happy; so, probably, it was all right.

Many times, people had come preaching, advocating, and proposing marriage proposals to Happy. Happy had looked at the pimps and realized that they were painting his side of the grass greener. Happy was always a fellow jumping the fence, so it really didn't bother him. Happy was probably, intrinsically happy!

Monk

Happy's shoulder had been jumped upon by a happy Capuchin monkey while on one of his journeys to the fish market by the moored boats. He had allowed the monkey to adopt him then and there, and had seriously named him Monk immediately.

Monk, as a baby, had arrived over the mountains from a small city to the seaside city on top of a circus bus. He had then escaped and scaled the tall and strong metaphorical boundary walls lining the seashore of the seaside city of life to have a good look at what lay beyond. He had glimpsed the horizon and never got down from the metaphorical walls, and then he had met his alter ego, Happy.

Thoughts went through Happy's mind as life progressed with Monk:

'In my room today I think I found truth in the billowing wings of my windows' yellow curtains, and the swinging doors opposite them, as they seemed to say, "Experience, but only the new," and in the golden yellow, I was not at all traumatized by my golden youth…

'The beauty of the pale green against the steel blue doesn't fade no matter what!

'It is we who have created everything within our universe, and it us who are scared of it…

'It is not I who is trying to find the solution, but it is I who is the answer.'

The rascal Monk made Happy so famous that they began to

be called by each other's names quite frequently. Happy was Monk, and Monk was Happy, but both were not happy always; for after all, no one can be always happy, especially if the burden of the world is placed upon their shoulders by naming them Happy and Monk!

Happy was a free, fearless, and original thinker; a capitalist entrepreneur to the core. He decided to settle down on a small island nearby with Monk, and named it, 'The Island of Monk Evolved'. He called the sea around it, 'The Sea of Humanity', and the lighthouse on it, in which he had his room at the top with Monk, 'Lighthouse of Beauty'.

On their first night together on their island, sitting by the sea on the sand under a coconut tree whose dark leaves sliced the cheese of the full moon, Happy whispered to Monk, "Soon, all the dumbasses will start coming here seeking wisdom from us. Any fool in isolation is presumed to be a wise man, a monk, by each one of these dumbasses, whom I will without uniqueness refer to as Dass, please do not laugh then Monk."

Happy had heard Monk screech, "Yes, Monk!"

Happy had then added under the stars on the small circular beach, "We will talk in staccato riddles, so that they will think they have understood, go away, not understand, and come back for more! Hehe!"

Monk had laughed heinously, and it had seemed to Happy, that his alter ego had asked, "What for all this monk Happy?"

Under the black universe pinpricked with blue, it was told to all and none in particular, "Because."

Happy was an artist, and soon had as his signboard for his lighthouse ashram, a printed board which had been cut out to show a cherubic bearded God with a halo hiding behind a cloud, in the center at the top, thinking, *'Did I create you or you created me!'* Facing God, a Capuchin monkey on the left side of the board's bottom, while on the right side of the bottom was an ass, Dass, laughing its guts out, and screaming, "Dass is monk's friend!"

Soon people on boats who had heard about the eccentric duo started coming in droves. It was love at first sight for eccentricity with divinity and humanity; a threesome!

Happy remained silent for a long time until people started depositing good scotch at his feet, and then broke his silence only to say thank you and drink wistfully looking at the sunsets on the horizon. It was only when a most exotic scantily clad female prostrated in front of him and begged him to partake of her offerings and answer her question, did he field his first question in front of a motley crew of admirers.

Happy had done his homework. He was a failed engineer but an intelligent, wise, and crafty one. He knew he could engineer the wise who came to him because they were foolish in seeking advice from others rather than from themselves after studying the world by themselves. He really knew how the wise became fools and fools wise.

During his long hours with scotch, provided by fools, he had sold some to the wise fishermen who came to party with him in the dark after all the fools had departed disappointed, and with their help, erected three medium sized screens in front of the lighthouse attached to a high-end laptop with Wi-Fi connection.

So, when the babe begged to ask her question at his feet, he said, "I name thee Babe, arise and ask!"

Babe happily got up at Happy's feet, and looking at both him and Monk, said, "They say Monk is evil, I say original sin, which is true O' happy monks?"

Monk chittered while Happy smartly fiddled with the keys

of his laptop. Suddenly, the three screens in front of the lighthouse and behind the monks sprang to life. The left screen showed Dass pointing at God and an image of Monk and saying while laughing heinously, "Monk is evil!"

On the middle screen, God, with a thunderbolt, was shouting, "Original sin!" while on the right screen, Monk was standing in front of a gene calmly saying, "No, it's my selfish gene."

For a second, all devotees stood stupefied and then started cheering, dancing, and howling wildly. Soon the sun set and the fishermen came back with the scotch they had bought to party with the fools knowing there was more in the well from which it was drawn.

The monks had spoken, and the next evening it was time for the second question. Two actors, who were lovers, came holding hands, and instead of asking, said firmly, "You are right monks, we are nothing but evolved animals!"

Soon a picture of two monkeys holding hands in front of the serpent on the Tree of Knowledge of Good and Evil flashed on the screens, followed by the previous day's image of Monk saying even more firmly, "Caution! Evolution should also mean moderation!"

Babe softly cried, "Monks, I only understand God, and not evolution, please help me. I am a dumbass!"

Monk closed his eyes with his hands while Happy said, "No Babe, you are a babe, but since you want to be a dumbass, I will fulfill your wish." Happy fiddled with his computer.

Monk on screen then said, "Dass doesn't understand that it took me millions of years to reach this stage." God sadly said, "Bye, then I am not needed…"

Dass on screen cried, "Stop fighting you two, evolution

should also mean compassion for me!"

Suddenly, a mule in a suit, an incongruous gentleman on the island beach, shot to his feet, "Monk, Happy, what is the right thing to do under any circumstance?"

Happy smiled, "That which helps life, as a single whole undivided organism, to evolve!"

Babe cried, "Thanks for completing the evolution puzzle Happy!"

Suddenly, two men, who had been discussing softly but agitatedly, got up, and started yelling at each other, "My religion is right!"

"No, mine!"

Happy said unhappily, "Dass brothers, you are in the same religion boat. Don't sink the others with your sticks of dynamite!"

A painter, who was drinking absinthe, got up, and shouted, "You are right monk Happy, these people are addicted to God, Eros, and Bacchus, but creativity is the only true addiction!"

Suddenly, a picture of Vincent Van Gogh flashed on the middle screen. The painter gulped more absinthe and radiated colors into the dying sunset.

A pregnant woman got up as the light was about to completely die and sighed, "It doesn't matter what we believe…"

Happy replied calmly, "No it doesn't, but your children will believe in what you believe, their children, their children, and so on… We will end up hairless apes fighting over planet-fruits."

The devotees and those that had come to scoff all lit a fire and began to dance a fierce dance at night.

Happy sighed at the sight of naked apes.

Suddenly, at midnight, there was fierce lightning!

The two lovers who were evolved animals started hugging,

kissing, and dancing wildly. They shouted at the lightning bolts in the sky, "O creator of life! Lightning into the primordial soup from which life arose! Bless us!"

Beautiful Babe, who, despite and because of her tremendous beauty, was all alone, shouted, "You are making a God out of lightning. What separates you two fools from me and the rest?"

It was clear to Happy that Babe was just a confused babe — confused between God and evolution.

Amidst the thundering, he said calmly to the motley crew around the fire, "Define anything, for example what you mean by God, and then talk about it please, but please, do not group and define. For example, don't classify men and women by their religions. Individuals are good or bad, individuals are both good and bad."

A timid westerner in a swimsuit asked, "Aren't God and lightning the same?"

Monk chittered and jumped on Happy's shoulder, who laughed into the fire, "Are they?"

A bold easterner shouted, "Energy! Energy! In lightning! The energy within my organic body is the Atman to the Brahman of universal energy! I am immortal!"

Monk covered his eyes with his paws. Happy laughed even harder, "The only immortality lies in work. But resume dancing all of you. It has not rained. No glory be to the skies or anybody else. Worship yourselves and be free!"

Dawn found everybody lying in the sand, except Happy who was meditating, looking into the colors of the rising sun, with Monk meditating on his shoulder.

The bold easterner shakily got up to his feet, removed a God object, incense, and a matchbox from his bag, and shouted into the sky, "God, I am lighting incense to worship you!"

Happy opened his non-existent third eye and said coldly, "Watch where you throw your matchstick. It should not light fire to the homes of others who are less fortunate than you, and have to live beside your posh villas in slums."

Babe, who had been jerked awake by this discussion, eagerly came towards Happy, knelt beside him, shooed away Monk who became angry, kissed Happy on his cheek gently, and said, "I had a dream. God has asked me to disprove him."

The delighted Happy laughed gently, "You are what I would call a confused atheist."

A chameleon ran across in front of the two. The easterner tried to hit it with a stone.

Babe proved herself delightfully intelligent as she said, "We are ultimate human beasts, aren't we?"

"Why?" growled the easterner.

"Because you stick to a color when it suits you and change colors when it doesn't!" laughed Happy.

This ruckus had awakened all by now, and they began another day in paradise.

Once, Monk had asked, "What for this, 'The Island of Monk Evolved', Happy?"

"Because," had replied Happy.

Happy had been vague then, but after the kiss by Babe, it had suddenly become clear to Happy that he had been chasing love with the help of money till then, but now he would be chasing love with the help of his philosophy. Happy was happy, for the money had not been his, but his father's, but at least his philosophy was his. He had a greater chance at true love now.

But this too was again philosophy, and there had been the death of a philosopher. Unfortunately, everything convoluted in life is philosophy. And even love is convoluted. It is not straight.

It is twisted like a corkscrew. So, what is straight, true, and beautiful in life? Simple, living life simply and as it comes. Happy had been doing just that on his island, talking whatever rubbish had come into his mind, philosophy, until of all the damned things in the world, Babe had come and kissed him. Love had suddenly tangled him up, and his philosophy was already tangling and untangling others. But Babe remained innocent. Innocence was her true beauty.

Happy, who had shooed away Monk and was sitting far away from all others too, where the waves almost died, in frothy water, realized that he was sinking again, in love! Beautiful women destroy destroyed philosophers! *'Nothing is sacred in life,'* thought Happy, as Monk came running back with Babe at his heels, in a delightful bikini. *'Philosophy is meant to be destroyed, otherwise love and life do not survive. Love and life have nothing to do with philosophy. Love is tangled, philosophy is too, and if both come together with life, they tangle up life too. This threesome is dangerous. Either philosophy or love should be kept out of life for life to survive! Anyway, life is going to get complicated with one of them, it had better not get totally messed up with both of them...'* thought Happy both sadly and happily. Babe planted another kiss on Happy's cheek.

With the second kiss came another revelation, revelation about a flaw in his reasoning. Happy had reasoned that he would chase love with the help of his philosophy, and also that love, philosophy, and life, formed an unholy threesome. So, Happy understood that he would have to set aside philosophy when it came to love with Babe in his life. But she desired his philosophy. Happy was caught in a quandary. This was the unholy triangle of which Happy's life formed one vertex. And the worst part was, Babe had only kissed him, not expressed her love for him.

Babe, who was now sitting down, purred, "Happy, don't be a perfect monk, teach me your philosophy."

Happy became a perfect ass, "Teach me love, Babe!"

She laughed, "Philosophy and love together! Don't be absurd!" She had both accepted and rejected. Women!

Babe asked, "Why don't you go out into the world and teach, Happy?"

The lover boy answered, "Babe, only the true seekers will seek, find, and understand anybody's teachings, I am but a nobody…"

Babe fiddled around in her purse, brought out a small mirror, beautified her face further, which was like extending infinity, and reaching further into her tiny purse, brought out a small smartphone. She fiddled with it and turning on a song, "Tell me there's a heaven…" asked Happy, pouting, "What is heaven, Happy?"

"Babe, men are hell bent on hell, for the sadomasochists, this desire to desire is heaven…"

"Why are you so negative, Happy?"

Monk screeched and ran away with Babe's purse, also snatching her smartphone from her hand while at it. Heaven came to an end.

Babe shouted, "Bad Monk!"

Happy laughed, "There is no good or evil in the universe Babe!"

"No?"

"No, Babe. There is none, but if you are wondering about butchers, terrorists, everything averages out in the universe, to zero, between life and death, like Mean Sea Level, water, the stuff of life, striving towards equilibrium like all elements in nature."

Babe sobered down, "Meaning of life, Happy?"

"Babe, what you want is what you get, period."

"Truth...?"

"The only truth is what you create to help you live till you die. Also, the only truth is that there is no truth in an unpredictable life, but to live that truth is dangerous for life..."

Babe broke down into sobs.

Happy knelt beside her, and wiping the tears from her soft cheeks, took her downward pointing determined chin in his fingers.

He raised her face towards his.

He wanted to kiss her on her full lips. But he had been philosophizing, and now he wanted some loving in his life, and on top of everything, he had made his love cry. What was he thinking?

Afternoon found him alone thinking about energy.

He knew, that energy was what you generated and experienced within, but energy could also be transmitted and received by a touch, a glance, a word... Physically or electronically. But Happy could not be certain. He knew it was dangerous to think of energy as something controlling environments and the people within them. He was becoming more and more sure that the world is contained within. A person's smile could be inscribed on one's mind as conniving or pleasing depending upon one's mood. And how does anything or anybody matter as long it doesn't affect one physically? By physically is also meant financially, so the whole gamut of life is played out physically. Money rules. And energy is tangible or intangible depending upon the effects it produces or not. Energy is tangible if it produces heat, or something else similar, and intangible if there is no medium to manifest it. Spiritual energy was therefore something very flimsy to Happy. You felt it if you wanted to, didn't if you didn't believe in it. You were the sun and the earth. This whole line of thought was troubling to Happy. He said to the universe under the hot sun, "We make or break within," and Monk came running to him. He got up with Monk on his shoulder and shouted to his devotees, "I don't want to be remembered. I want to live!"

Everybody decided to make and have a hearty lunch with scotch as an appetizer.

After lunch, time found Happy, happy. He knew life was all about you, you and you alone. Others were there, but others were themselves, by themselves. Nobody mattered to another except where money was concerned, or else in other ways where nothing except money was the common denominator. Others hid from this fact, but Happy reveled in its revelation of it to him. Life was dead as far as empathy was concerned. His devotees were flocking to him because they wanted to party with a clear conscience, telling themselves that they were on the search for truth. He would kickass them the truth!

Early evening found him sitting in front of his screens with Monk.

The absinthe artist came carrying a loaded gun pointed to his head. Babe had started screaming. The artist said, "Life is meaningless without God, a divine purpose behind it. I, an atheist, am tired…"

Happy said grimly, "Life itself means its continuation, procreation. Greatest meaning is in every moment, your perfection! Get married and have kids.

"You are an artist, absinthe man. Life is the greatest art. It has painting, poetry, music…"

The artist screamed, "What about singing one's same old song? Dancing to someone else's tune? I am tired!"

"Don't kill yourself. Be good!" shouted Happy.

"Why be good?"

"Be good for goodness' sake. Beauty doesn't need anything else to complete it. Life is beautiful. Live it dead man!"

"I don't have a holy book to live life by!" screamed the dying man.

"To an atheist, to the unholy, holy books are great philosophies and literature, nothing less and nothing more! Live in reality O' artist!"

"I can't. I am not famous like you monk Happy. I am a poor artist. I do not have what you have. You have guts to fight and claim fame!"

"It takes guts not to fight and suffer, O' gentle man..."

The artist had fallen to his knees.

"Rise and paint the sunset!

"You don't need fame to be famous to your friends. One good friend is worth a billion others who are not. Bring out your palette of friends and paint beautiful friendships on the canvas of life."

The artist put down his gun and reached for his absinthe.

Happy laughed, and a depressed Greek philosopher in front of a noose, and a happy donkey running to eat a carrot dangling in front of it from a stick tied to its back, both appeared side by side on the screens. He bellowed, "Instead of becoming wise and stopping, it is better to stay foolish and continue!"

The artist, gulping absinthe, shouted, "Only those who have beauty inside can appreciate beauty outside," and sat down to paint the sunset.

The lovers approached Happy. They were arguing with each other as to who was the better actor. They asked in unison, "What is an equal relationship Happy?"

Happy thundered, "That the minority and majority hate each other. Thinkers like me and dancers like you moving to each other's moves!"

"God will punish you for being so candid Happy!" shouted the lovers.

"No! The naked ape will. Karma is between naked apes. It is nothing divine!" laughed Happy at the very scantily clad duo, as Monk, clothed in fur, came running up to his shoulder.

The mule in a suit, who had approached quietly without being noticed, bent down in front of Happy and whispered, "Thank you for this knowledge monk Happy. With greater knowledge comes greater wealth."

"Burden!" shouted the suddenly enlightened actors.

"Wisdom?" seemed to ask Monk with his tail raised in the form of a question mark.

Happy had closed his eyes in silence.

Babe came running over with a book in her beautiful hand. She plunked down beside Happy, and putting one arm over his shoulders, with the other pushing her book in his face, purred, "Happy dear, what is infinite regress?"

Happy sighed, "Greater complex creator…"

The mule laughed, "Bigger better deal!"

Monk had his question mark tail.

The mule proved himself a philosopher. He said to Happy, "Mystics understand the origin, life, and demise of the universe. Shoonya: nothing to something to everything!"

Happy proved himself a rhymer, "The words mystic and logic rhyme, but to positively correlate them is a crime!"

"You are a lucky naked ape Happy," said the mule looking at Babe across Happy.

"I am lucky because if not for others' mistakes, I would have committed them, Dass," laughed Happy.

"What do you mean babe?" asked Babe.

"Nothing you should worry your pretty little head about, Babe."

The mule laughed, "Is such a naked ape successful?"

"If they call him crazy, then certainly," smiled Happy running a hand through Babe's hair.

Happy looked at a pastel horizon, and Babe asked, "What are you looking at dear?"

"My mind, emptying it of judgements over time…"

The mule sighed, "I have seen life Happy. You call me Dass. I know what you mean by Dass, dumbass. One day, you will pay for your thinking."

"If freedom is not free, then what is?" sighed Happy into the horizon.

"I am rich," said the mule. "The moneyed believe in God. You don't."

"Can money measure someone's true worth, Dass?"

"All right Happy, almost all believe in God!"

"Can truth be made a matter of statistics, Dass?"

The mule gave up. He shouted exasperatedly with both arms held high, "What fool lives in an ideal world?"

Happy kissed Babe, "Only Love!"

Night fell, fire raged, and naked apes drank, ate, and danced.

Dawn birthed a beautiful hermaphrodite on The Island of Monk Evolved. She was of the type Alexander liked. Happy was immediately attracted towards her. In the rising sun, she introduced herself as, "Butterfly." Happy immediately dubbed her "Butt". Babe was happily amused, but jealous too, looking at Happy's happy face.

Butt asked, "Can beauty be found in disorder, in a disordered world? In asymmetry? Does beauty need symmetry? Perfection? Conformance to norms? Is beauty a symmetrical flawless face and figure? Can there be perfection in imperfection?"

Happy asked, mesmerized by perfect imperfection, "Does the beauty of a poem depend upon symmetry and rhyming? Or the pains and pleasures of the experiences of the poet?"

She asked, "Is beauty subjective or objective? Is it the same for all?"

Happy answered with a question, "Isn't everything subjective? Isn't objective science useless in assigning purpose to a third human sex? How are you useful for evolution? You are useful only for your beauty in perfect imperfection not suited to the beauty of utility of evolution! I love you. My beauty is subjective, and definitely, it is not the same for all…"

Butterfly beautiful planted a kiss on Happy's forehead and Babe flamed up!

The hermaphrodite was wise. She said, "Correlate my situation with Shoonya, monk Happy."

Happy was happy to oblige, "Everything matters and nothing matters. Symmetry matters and asymmetry doesn't. It is the mindset with which one looks at anything which can be an object of beauty. The beauty of the object depends upon the beauty of the subject. It is not about how to appreciate external beauty, but how to become internally beautiful, so you can appreciate all. The problem of an ugly world is solved and everything becomes beautiful. This is my personal to the universal, Butt!"

The beautiful and wise hermaphrodite broke down in the glorious morning on the island beach. "Beauty begins with the mother. Mother nature, mother earth. Everything evolves but beauty remains unchanged and eternal. To a neanderthal mother, its child was beautiful and vice versa. How can I, who cannot become a mother, be beautiful and happy, Happy?"

Happy said softly, "You are beautiful. Taking a cue from Dostoevsky, do not attempt to base beauty and happiness on the dictates of reason and logic."

Butt rushed up and hugged Happy. All, who had come to watch, admire, or scoff, all devotees and miscreants alike, were watching incredulously, all except the jealous Babe who was an angry red.

Happy got to his feet from where he was sitting, admiring the dawn of a glorious new morning on the island beach, another dawn, another dawn, and spoke to his flock, with Butt clinging on to his thigh, "Beauty cannot be defined, but it can be experienced by undefining oneself. Two bodies become one for greater beauty. One becomes one with beauty.

"We have drawn the beauty of symmetry from the universe, from symmetric planets, stars, and orbits, but we cannot get outside of the universe to assess its symmetry. Everything is subjective, from within the universe, and therefore, symmetry, though a beautiful part of beauty, cannot claim sole ownership of beauty.

"Do not judge Butt, Butterfly…

"Why aren't you working, assholes? I am…

"Inner beauty can be created only by beautiful work. It is the only way to really live in the moment. Such a moment is the most beautiful eternity in which only the beautiful past and wonderful future we are creating for ourselves flow into. Usually, only the unnecessary dead past and an uncontrollable future play havoc with and in the moment.

"If one understands that one is just an organism, whose consciousness, its resulting pains and pleasures, of relationships, for we are nothing but other humans, are just a particular association of atoms, it does not remove beauty, but adds to the beauty of the universe, and we are the universe. With this understanding, there is no more the pain of death, death of so many unnecessary things, but only the joy of being one with the universe.

"Butt is the universe!

"She is amalgamated beauty!

"Truth and beauty."

A saint had come on the heels of the hermaphrodite; a villain.

He said, "You are drunk in the dawn Happy. I will not call you monk.

"Can the highest ideal, truth, be found in beauty?"

Happy laughed, "Welcome soldier!

"Does truth favor the serenity of a saint or the arrogance of a drunk? Truth should be a constant and effortless way of life. What helps it to become so? Alcohol? God? Both? None?"

Happy turned to the absinthe artist who was watching him, and spoke fiercely, "Starry Starry Night is the beauty of madness, the madness inherent in all men of passion; the lovers, the sufferers. Placid people will think only of blank pools; however, that beauty is for another time and place. A calm sage staring into wisdom. The true Narcissus. But! There is no difference between truth and beauty, and all is subjective! There is no objective right or wrong darling saint! No one can judge me or Monk! We do and live as we please! Partake of our celebrations, or prepare to be roasted alive on words of wisdom which are hotter than the coals of hell!"

He then grabbed Butt and kissed the Butterfly passionately. Babe was hotter than the words of wisdom coals.

It was a threesome of three sexes.

Monk was confused and sat eating banana after banana.

Happy had died. It had been the death of a philosopher. He had gone zany and started his island ashram. Now, it was obvious to him, and him alone, that he had become stark raving mad. But to all the others, he was the guru of gurus. A guru is measured with respect to his followers, and if they are low, he is bound to be high, and all followers are low. That is why a leader is placed on a pedestal. But one should not think that Happy was anything other than wise, for it is only the wise who know that anything you say is bound to be appreciated by at least one person somewhere, and if you have enough followers, all that you say goes. One can say anything and be profound to the masses. It is just about somehow making it to the top by being arcane and abstruse. The whole world loves a mystery. Happy knew that all is truth and all is false in the universe. One man's meat is another man's poison. It is just convincing some that meat is poison and others vice versa. People will eat, swallow anything preached to them from a podium. Happy knew this and was wise. But he, even though he knew that there was no right or wrong in the universe, was not bad. He knew there was no good or bad, but he was good. It was simply because he was being honest with himself and preaching to others what he himself practiced. There was no hypocrisy in Happy, and he was in love with Babe and Butt simultaneously.

It was possible.

Monk was left alone with his bananas.

Lunch was over and Happy sat with Babe to his right and Butt to his left in front of the screens in front of the lighthouse, facing his devotee gang which was growing larger by the hours.

The actor lover said, "I am the new Romeo. My love is great," and kissed his lover.

Happy laughed, "Hurt will be too. The price of pleasure, which is pain, is always high!"

"Well said Happy!" shouted an eccentric long-haired young writer in tatters. He started copying down Happy's words in a dirty diary.

The mule asked him loudly, "Why don't you use a device and your own words young man?"

Pat came the artistic reply, "One like-minded quill is worth a thousand devices! Now, these are my own words added to the words of a master!"

Happy felt a warm glow within him for the poor young writer. He smiled beatifically at him.

The new Romeo asked, "Why does the chicken cross the road, Happy?"

"You foolish naked ape! You keep worrying about the poor chicken crossing the road because you are a masochist who loves the pain arising out of the desire to make sense out of senseless things!"

"Sorry Happy! Please teach me. If you want, I will also teach you what I know in lieu of fees!" whimpered the actor.

Happy became stern, "Certainly. One can always learn from another, but frivolity should be an escape from philosophy and not vice versa."

It was again evening. Again, a beautiful evening! For, how can it be anything other than beauty and romantic sunsets in paradise!

There would be talk about beauty.

Butt had ensured that and Babe had sealed the deal unnecessarily further.

All the Dasses sat like disciples.

Monk was tired of eating bananas.

Butt wiggled in front of the lighthouse of beauty, and asked, "Happy and Monk, were you happy all alone on your Island of Monk Evolved?"

"Fly away Butterfly. If someone can give you happiness, they can take it away too. The only real happiness is one which is self-contained!"

Butt became sulky, and Babe happy.

"You can't control them Happy!" came a jeering shout from the audience from one of those who had come to scoff.

Wise Butt tried to stem the flow of obnoxious waters, "Happy, does free will exist? Doesn't the Butterfly Effect of physics prove that a single thought can affect billions and vice versa? Physics proves free will doesn't exist!"

"Butt, the very fact that you can argue about free will and the fact that you are arguing about free will both proves and disproves its existence. Assume you have free will and help those who are unable to help themselves... Okay?"

"How can I help you Happy in this time of a pandemic?"

"Butt, in times of pandemics, for those who fear death, inside is beauty, and for those who love life, outside is beauty, but I am one with no outside and inside. Fly, Butt, fly... Butterfly..."

Butterfly was wise. It was night now, which had suddenly set in. All the irrelevant ones had quickly left to party. The hermaphrodite understood that when Happy had said that he was one with no outside and inside, he had meant the universe. She was looking for a pattern in life in which she could fit. So, he asked Happy, "Happy, what are patterns in the universe?"

Happy was relaxing. Babe was a little away from him and playing with Monk. He said, "Patterns are common results arising in the workings of uncommon minds which seem uncommon to common minds... Choose your sex constellation and become a star member Butt…"

"People treat me like wood Happy," burst out Butt.

"The door of my lighthouse is more beautiful than the person who walks through it, Butt. You want to know why? It is because, I cannot hate the impersonal door unless I bang my head on it, and even then, I would be wrong to hate and not simply love."

"But your wood is good. I love you even more than my impersonal door. You have become far too personal for me in the space of a single day, love!"

Babe came rushing hearing the word 'love', and put a question at night, "Why are sunsets and sunrises beautiful for all, honey?"

Happy, who was lying beside a fire blazing like a night sun, answered lazily, "Babe, it is because they are impersonal and occur each and every day punctually and are free for all everywhere!"

He then swigged from his scotch and was free of both Babe and Butt.

Some half-hearted policemen came with the soft dawn sun hearing wild reports of obscene partying on the island, to take stock of the whole matter, but upon seeing the blissful Happy meditating into the rising sun with Monk immersed in it too, they were completely mesmerized by what they experienced and began to talk about it in respectful hushed tones as the spiritual energy of the island. They observed the carefully built pyramid of scotch and absinthe bottles, and revered them as offerings to the gods drunk by holy men. They saw scantily clad men and women and worshipped them as true devotees braving the elements. Thus ended the only brief scrape of Happy and Monk on their island with the law of the land.

Movement

Men and women had begun to stay and sleep on the island since some time. Provisions came for them. More devotees had been coming every day and most staying. It had become slightly crowded, but the weather was delightful, and all slept on the sand under the stars. Happy and Monk sometimes retreated to their room at the top of the lighthouse — to be far from the madding crowd. But almost always there were electric question and answer sessions. Life was charged on The Island of Monk Evolved on which there was the Lighthouse of Beauty throwing light upon The Sea of Humanity.

After breakfast, Happy was strolling with Butt and Babe on either side of him with Monk playing around their meandering legs. An eccentric scientist with frizzy hair was joining them from a distance.

Butt asked, slipping her hand into Happy's right hand, "Happy, why do people both love and hate beauty? Are they crazy?"

"No, my dear Butterfly, simply jealous. It is all about what they want but can't have — beautiful people and things, movie stars and fast cars."

Babe slipped her hand into Happy's left, "Explain hate and jealousy with respect to beauty, Happy…"

"When some people hate a model, who is beautiful to others, they call the model ugly because of their jealousy, Babe."

The eccentric scientist, who was wearing a white lab coat

over a swimsuit, and who had overheard the three, came running up on bowed legs, and shrieked, "So, why do people hate an ugly scientist Happy?"

"Because, sir, the ugly scientist sticks to beautiful hard harsh facts, while the morons want him to toe the God and religion line!"

"Explain beauty with respect to evolution, Happy," pleaded the man of science.

"Let me tell you the ugly truth about beauty. Evolution, which demands survival, asks from beauty, duty, symmetry to be useful in survival, symmetry necessary for smooth motion, for what is stagnant is dead, and only change life."

The scientist added, "Chaos, if looked at from afar, is symmetrical. A molecule looked at from close range is too. It is in the middle of human life we get confused!"

Happy broke out into a haiku:

"Kingfisher in wild

Because of vibrant beauty

Can't escape duty"

The tired old scientist asked, "Does a parched child in Africa understand your concentrated solution of beauty Happy? Will there be God for it in it?"

"God and beauty are a dichotomy sir, even pain and death are beautiful if all conditionings are removed."

Happy soon distanced himself from everybody, even Monk, whom he chased away with thrown sand, and sat on a rock on the beach.

He had suddenly realized that the death of a philosopher had not been complete. For it to be complete, and he free of even himself, a himself which held his past and all its problems, he had to completely stop doing all that he had been doing his whole life, whether consciously or unconsciously, which was philosophizing, necessarily or unnecessarily. He had to stop being Happy to become happy. He would have to make a clean break with all that he was, his aspirations, desires, and fears. He would have to stop loving Butt and Babe too. But how? Become ordinary. And, to become ordinary, for the extraordinary, is extraordinarily difficult. To be happy in an ordinary world, one has to be ordinary, otherwise, it will eat the extraordinary one alive. That is why Happy was on an island with other eccentrics of his kind. The mainland would have nothing to do with any of them. But Happy wanted to go and live on the mainland. This was the problem.

Happy was not left alone by his devotees. They came and surrounded the rock on which he sat. Their butts were wet in the sand and they were happy and eager for wisdom.

The lovers asked, "Happy, can the highest ideal, truth, be found in beauty?"

"Actors, the only truth is beauty, but it is not exactly the same for all. There are innumerable nuances. Even the same word is not understood in the same way by you very two."

The old scientist would not let up, "Happy, again, can a starving child in Africa appreciate sunsets?"

"Sir, again, sunsets are free for all, everywhere, and are regularly punctual beauties which can be enjoyed by both the suppressor and the suppressed, freeing both from tyranny."

"You are ludicrous Happy, your philosophy knows only the hunger of the intellect, but not that of the stomach!"

"Ideas are ludicrous, sir. Consider the logical alphabets A, B, and C which may combine to give the illogical word BAC, just like logical thoughts got permuted and combined into the illogical idea of GOD. This is what keeps men evil and children hungry."

Butt and Babe purred, "Your thoughts leap across seemingly unbridgeable chasms, from and to seemingly unrelated peaks of thought. How? And why?"

"Butt, two cheeks of a person are related even though they can't see each other. They have to be slapped to make the person realize she has complementary ones. Babe, your cheeks are pretty too. Turn!"

Happy drank that night. He remembered when he had been offered girls in fields by drunkards in bars. He had thought, *'Was flesh worth the mind?'* and had answered, *'Yes'*. But now he was caught in fleshy mind, whatever that might mean. *'Is man separate from his flesh? Is the mind hallowed?'* screamed Happy's mind.

He was caught amidst bodies, flesh. Confused twisting flesh. Life is flesh. Sweating screaming painful flesh. Anybody who is a body and refuses to accept the fact of flesh is a hypocrite.

Happy had understood men and women. They are twisted miasmas of flesh. Gurus are assholes trying to analyze the unanalyzable anal. The second place where nerves are most active. They are perverts. Anybody who tries to analyze is a pervert; according to language.

Live was the watchword. Mad was the byword. Happy screamed in his sleep, "Men cannot be redeemed. They are bound for hell on earth."

Happy was sad.

Happy was a failed lover, not because he had failed to love, but because he had failed to get. And therefore, he decided, on that night, that he would not only stop asking for love, but would also stop giving love.

Once the route is closed, there is no room for pain too.

The next morning found Happy in a further enlightened state of mind.

He had known that devotees want wisdom and gather it from the nonsense of philosophers. That the devotees themselves know and have what they want, but want a certain someone to officialize it for them.

Happy himself had been the devotee of obnoxious philosophers and their philosophies. He knew none of them led anywhere. But here he was, leading none, and going nowhere.

He was happy.

People are lost. They don't know where. They don't look, but think, lost in their minds, without ascertaining their surroundings. They look to philosophers whose life is different from theirs, and hope to find a solution.

Happy was out to kill that thought of a philosopher having tried to die one.

Happy thought with the star of a sun, *'Life is a billion stars exploding and trying to spread their nuances among their smithereens... Life is the trajectory of a butterfly, nectar, sweeter, which flower?*

'Impossible to define life, so whither philosophy? There is a simple equation, Life = Death, but it stinks of pessimism. So, let there be no rightful philosophy nonsense. I will give these idiots what we both like, nonsense, and let us all be blissfully happy in a nonsensical world!'

A fanatic from one region of the world came in his colored dress followed by Happy's other devotees hating this newcomer. He fell at Happy's feet and sought a solution to the world's problems by asking about other fanatics from other parts of the world, "What about progeny procreated in excess by fanatics Happy?"

Happy's soft morning sun was marred by a spot. "They want to reproduce their illogical mental ideologies in physical numbers to have both brawn and convoluted brains in threatening numbers. A hardened tree breaks when bent. Grown men cannot be converted. Green grass children are grown to ensure compliance, bending, so that they can grow into bent, twisted, hard, and threatening trees which don't provide shade but firewood to burn the world. You are a fanatic too. Get off The Island of Monk Evolved. You have not evolved. Maybe neither have I, for to talk of such rot is to speed up the spread of such rot."

"Please let me stay, I will convert."

"Conversion is one thing we do not do here, but you can stay, for who am I anyway to deny a man a place on Earth?"

Love made its appearance, or rather lost love.

The sun was warm. All were sitting comfortably upon the beach, and a handsome fellow started crying, "I miss my girl who has left me Happy…"

Happy sighed into the breaking waves, "You are both atoms kissing each other through others in the universe, Moth. I will call you Moth, because your mood is dark like the night, and yet you are in search of light. You are here, but don't burn in my flame. Be a light unto yourself, and you will not burn."

Moth smiled, "Yes, a splendid material body including the so-called spiritual is but atoms, Happy…—"

The waves crashed in the cool morning.

"But live the illusion, Moth, you will die happily. As I always say, 'It is better to stay foolish and continue than to become wise and stop'."

Moth laughed with most.

The absinthe artist piped up, "Happy, why does the world

love to see an artist in misery?"

"Van Gogh cut off his ear for a prostitute. You better just have fun and don't do anything stupid. Now to answer your question. For humans, it is not that they have to be happy, but happier than competitors."

Happy laughed, "Hey, Butt, crack up on this!" and turning saw Butt and Babe, who were eyeing the handsome Moth, and laughed louder.

The fanatic had softened. He asked, "Sorry Happy, but why am I happy seeing a person in misery?"

The waves thundered.

"Dass, you are like Hitler, trying to be happier at the cost of making misery for others."

The fanatic hardened, "So, are you trying to say you are the only saint, Happy?"

The waves died at the beach like all good and bad.

Happy smiled, "Absolutely not, Dass, actually the opposite, for a true saint is an absolute non-interferer who lives off roots and fruits in forests away from all, but here I am, with all the stuff I need, and you too!"

"Just whom are you trying to impress with all your impractical philosophy, Happy?"

"Dass, one always wants to impress only one's high school sweetheart, the one that got away, no matter how many trophies one has. It is just the *Will to Power* which is nothing but the *Will to Pleasure!*"

"Happy!" screamed Butt.

"Fly away Butterfly! Escape from this philosophy and psychology. Fly away Moth! Don't squeal Babe."

Butt cried, "You became a philosopher, a Shoonya, after losing all Happy. I have learnt about you before coming here.

Was it worth it?"

Happy became sad, "Absolutely not Butt, I wish I was a bum like you. Understanding humanity in all its inhumanity destroys one's humanity."

Butt clutched Moth, "I don't want to be like you Happy. I want to die a carefree whimsical butterfly!"

Happy smiled widely, "Butt, understand this simple line. 'How you live is how you die'. So, live happily my love, fly!"

With this talk of freedom, the fanatic became fanatical. He screamed, "You call the hermaphrodite, Butt, instead of Butterfly, you ask Babe the pig not to squeal, and you call us Dasses for dumbasses, what right do you have bloody monk Happy?"

Monk started screeching. After all, he was an evolved ape. He had come to be at the side of his master. He knew all were servants of one or another.

Happy laughed. Laughter dissolves. He said, "Butt is good for we are all bums and love bums. We are all pigs who love to wallow in the squalor of our misery. We are all dumbasses for we are not mules. Not castrated by birth but self-castrated after. Anything more, Dass?"

Laughter did not dissolve the fanatic. He shouted, "You are a masochistic pervert who loves to watch his girl and hermaphrodite frolic with another male!"

Happy smiled as Monk ran away from him, "What is ours?"

Happy sat alone till evening when he received a letter from home. One in a long line of secret correspondences. He read it with a stoic apathy like Marcus Aurelius would have.

Happy had always travelled the best places, the best bars, drunk the best scotch, and had staunchly believed that his happiness lay solely in himself and nowhere else.

But the journey had required money, his father's, and that

had been the death of a philosopher.

But now, would the journey of a non-philosopher be complete without money? And what exactly is meant by completion? Death? If so, he could commit suicide and be free, be complete! But completion lies in non-completion. That's what keeps a man or woman going and complete. Happy had to travel until he could travel no further, until that ability was taken away from him.

So, should he forsake money or accept it? Was he allowed to decide, or was it just a whim of a spoiled son? Would his father accept the death of a philosopher and make him an ordinary man?

Life has no answers.

Happy had mentally come to a place where he used to come with his love, his only love, his high school sweetheart who was his only heart, and he was philosophizing. Death. Again. Again, the truth was he wanted to become ordinary, get married and leave all his loves to the wolves.

Would Happy's life be happy with arranged love, for that was all his people knew, and Happy was not his people.

Happy was terrified yet delighted, for the unknown was beckoning him, a scary unknown. And he would jump. Yes, he would take a plunge into the abyss and hope it would reverse and open, dropping him into heaven.

The Island of Monk Evolved would be Happy's last hurrah, shouted in the midst of the infidels of society. He would no more have the courage to sift through the annals or anals of philosophy. He would be caught in a humdrum, a beautiful lullaby of sleep from life's wonders. Philosophy is bullshit, but at least it stinks. It is alive unlike staid life. *'What are we without philosophy?'* was Happy's last clutch at the straw of insanity which is better than any straw of sanity. He was drowning in life!

Happy had come to an epiphany, that, "Philosophy and earning do not go together," and that was the death of a philosopher.

Happy never meditated. He once had but realized it was a curse. It made one feel disconnected from the world, and one never was, until dead. *'What foolhardiness!'* thought Happy, *'Fools!'*

Happy meditated, *'Scotch is God!'* and felt happy.

Happy knew that if he died of the unhappy virus, his friend, Selene, with whom he had been communicating since the beginning, his twin, would complete his story for him: story of life, story of a misled life, story of a life fully tried to have been lived, with loves and prostitutes, it did not matter. A story is a story. Half or complete. Everybody wants their own ending to stories. So, why deny somebody their own happy ending, even if yours may have not been one? That is the hallmark of a true story. Unfinished.

Happy stared at the sunset. He was with Butt who had come back from wherever she had been. She asked, "Are sunsets the only thing you love to stare at?"

There was a glow on Happy's face, lighting up the setting sun, as he said, "More than sunsets, I love to stare at hate on the face of a betrayer and see love!"

Butt fidgeted and Happy astutely changed the subject, "I love to say, 'Love you', to everybody at the end of a telephone conversation."

"Will you say that when I call you?"

"After you and Babe leave with Moth, I will say, 'Love you', to all three of you if and whenever you call me."

Butt started crying and begged, "Let me leave with your biggest philosophy…"

"If you are happy in the present moment, your whole past, life, is made right."

"Thank you. Babe and Moth asked me to bid goodbye to you on their behalf. They did not have the nerve to meet you before we all left."

"I understand. My philosophy is not for all; probably for no one else other than myself. Everybody is slowly getting unsettled. It is simply because I am not telling them what they want to hear. Listen, I too will probably not stay long here. Home is calling me. All these paradise islands are but passing fancies in life. The only home is where your family is. You too go and make a home with the one you really love and who understands you."

"You loved and understood me, Happy. Why can't I love you back in the same way?"

"Unfortunately, a great truth of life is that we do not love those who love us. We are always looking for a bigger, better deal and consider those who love us to be below us simply because they love us. Actually, those who love us are not simply below us, they are at the bottom of the food chain, they are the scum of the earth because they love. Fly Butt, fly."

"But you state that a mortal being's only goals are to eat, mate, and survive, right, Happy?"

"Yes, Butt, only those who have a death wish like me are gods."

"So, if only those who have a death wish are gods, are terrorists' gods too, you so-called philosopher?"

"You have every right to hate me. After all you are leaving me. Now, to answer your question, Butt, you are a bum, terrorists believe in God, so they are not gods."

"So, what advice do you have for ordinary mortals like us, Happy?"

"For those whose neurons don't fire well enough, I say sprinkle some spirit on them!"

Happy got up. Monk came running in from the dusk.

Happy said, "Goodbye, I am off to douse my neurons in scotch and forget the new threesome of you, Babe, and Moth. Please leave before you change your mind. I and this Island of Monk Evolved have the ability to make minds evolve. If you stay long enough you will start loving me for real and all your desires will become tormented. Good night. I see your boat has come."

Happy walked towards freshly blazing fires and danced with a bottle of scotch, all alone, as he had always been.

Happy fell down!

He wondered, 'Was love membrane and mucus as Marcus had said! Or much more!'

Was his love meant to be wasted in the rat holes of time? He had loved, but was it lust? Was he after a virgin body or a virgin mind? Aren't both the same?

He was supposed to get hitched now, but what remained pure? Love was lost with youth.

Youth, what is youth? A mistake! You have it but don't love it. He had loved the girl whose name was Money. Money was beautiful, a fragrance of a mango tree in the summer. He had wanted the fruit and had plucked but not eaten it. What a fool he was! Monk would have arrived.

Happy was a monkey unevolved.

He didn't know the value of money or the things it bought.

Happy screamed into the midnight, "Money! Money is the only salt of the earth."

He didn't know himself with respect to money.

Money had wanted money. His father had it, but Happy didn't. That had been the death of a philosopher.

This was the dirt all had been leading towards.

Therefore, Happy wanted no more philosophy, no more analysis, he wanted an end to all love and philosophy. He was determined to have a stupid life, and he would have it.

"Damn," said Happy, and that was what he would do to lead a damned life.

Life was dirt and he would add stink to it.

Happy slept a troubled sleep.

He woke up refreshed and ashamed.

He had written to Selene when drunk and hoped she would understand.

The dawn was beautiful.

All the hurt was gone.

After the night of mad thoughts, Happy had become a calm warrior. It was the calm after the storm. He was waiting for a samurai warrior who had asked for an audience with him. Happy had become quite famous.

The sea was a cool blue like the sky. The sea was almost empty of white waves and the sky of white clouds. The breeze was cool and brisk.

Soon, warrior met warrior on the sands of time. The man of sword greeted Happy with, "I train so that the sword fights on its own."

Happy, the writer, poet, and philosopher, answered, "So also the pen, mind."

The warrior with the sword bowed deeply, "The sword kills. It doesn't know the enemy, but only that the enemy is the enemy."

The warrior with the pen and mind replied, "Yes, atoms don't have right or wrong."

Happy could be called a Zen master if not anything else. His mind matched with that of the man with the sword from Japan.

"So, Happy, according to you, we are kissing and killing across space and time without rhyme or reason…"

"Again, atoms, men, and women have blinded themselves by opening their eyes to the forbidden fruit from the tree of knowledge of good and evil…"

The sun shone weakly.

The warrior asked, "Isn't good right and bad wrong?"

"Only in an ideal world, for it is good to kill your enemy but not right to kill a human!"

The calm warrior drew his sword and tested the might of Happy's mind, "You, you who espouse evolution, say you are God, how, you enemy of reason! I will slice you!"

"I never said I was God. People on this island are calling me God. I do not want it or anything else except money and scotch. Anyway warrior, being God means not having faults within one, being able to love all completely. Sorry, I am not God, for I despise the ways of men!"

The warrior smiled and sheathed his sword, and then added sadly, "I can't grab your thoughts, Happy."

Happy laughed by the blue sea, "I am the blade of the sword, not the hilt."

"Mine is a samurai sword," laughed back the warrior.

Happy continued the laughing tennis match, "Mine is a superconducting sword. It has no resistance to killing bad ideas!"

Laughter reached a deuce.

The warrior told strongly, "Greatness takes effort!"

"No, suffering," said Happy sadly.

"Greatness eludes or resides in one?" asked the Japanese.

"Depends upon how one over one's sword presides, to kill or be killed by inner demons," said the writer, poet, and still philosopher softly.

An Indian Bengal tiger had joined them. He had painted himself in yellow stripes, and upon finding a silence between the two warriors, the animal roared, "I like to improvise!"

Happy laughed. He liked to laugh. He said, "To wing it, you first need wings! If pigs had wings, they would fly! Have you read Wodehouse O tiger? Stripes don't make tigers. Zebras have them too. Take a bath."

But it was a wise tiger who wanted talk of a different kind. He said, "Isn't it a vector from past to future?"

Happy was ready, He said, "Sorry, I misjudged you. Let us come to philosophy from comedy, though I believe comedy should be the only philosophy. Well, coming to your question, yes, it is a vector from past to future; however, you can't escape opposite vectors. Future to past should be from happiness to sadness and vice versa for both, otherwise, the vector is not a vector, but directionless."

The animal roared, "I have come to you Happy, because I find that all humans are inhuman!"

"True, none can resist hating, try, and if you succeed, fly, wing it!"

The tiger was getting confused, "Happy, what exactly is philosophy?"

The sea roared with fresh waves, and Happy answered, "Philosophy is self-suffocated inherent need for hedonism morphed into intellectualism. Ask emperor Marcus Aurelius…"

"Then can I do whatever I want?" roared the animal.

"As long as you can get away with it, why not? What do you think the successful are doing?"

"Zonk it monk Happy! What exactly according to you is the meaning of life?"

"Meaningless death, now stop hunting for answers O' tiger!"

"How many lonely tears have I shed in jungles of solitude!" wept the tiger suddenly.

"You could have watered the nonexistent gardens of Eden O' puss of loss!"

Suddenly the warrior from Japan asked, "Why should I keep bowing, Happy? I am tired of my tradition."

"Keep bowing because everybody dies now and then and then forever. Keeps your sword humble."

"To whom do you bow, Happy?"

"To my father who can no more see humanity sunk," sighed Happy looking at a fisherman's boat on the sea.

There was scotch. The tiger drank. He softly said, "I think you are a loveless philosopher fool, Happy."

Happy took a swig too. "Pussy, every second of my life is part of an endless love letter to her."

Another drag by the tiger, and then the words, "You are Romeo, Happy!"

"Why not puss of loss. All philosophical and moral books can and should be filled with only one word, 'love'."

"I rest my case on you Happy."

"I won't judge, puss of loss."

The warrior spoke, "I have to live up to all my great past achievements."

The dying philosopher replied, "An unconditioned individual is free of both great and small past acts. You don't have to live up to anything you have done, for the small past comes with the great past…"

"How to stop hate, Happy?" asked the animal.

"Puss of loss, opposites resurrect each other. To stop hate, you must stop love. Forget it!"

The warrior from Japan queried, "So, since happiness brings

with it sadness, where and when can peace be found, Happy?"

Happy sang with the soft blue waves, "If not in the here and now, nowhere anytime, sirs."

The tiger asked, "Everybody talks about living in the moment, but none do. Is it so difficult Happy?"

"Yes, puss of loss, living in the moment takes a lifetime to master and a moment to lose… It is like being a grain of sand in eternity."

The warrior sighed, "I feel so old. Teach me before it's too late, Happy."

"Youth is always a lost kingdom for the wise, O' warrior. The wise teach themselves by keeping all their senses open, always. You know this. You don't need me. Now go home. Fight life."

The warrior got up.

The tiger too got up and said, "Teach me something great before I too take your leave Happy."

"Here you go. You don't have to explain yourself to anybody, not even to yourself. Now run off puss of loss."

The warrior bowed, and taking a cue from him, after a second, the tiger too.

Happy had closed his eyes.

The band disbanded.

It was sunset, when all negative thoughts come to be drowned in the placid pool of positivity.

Happy submerged, 'I want my own family, and that family will want God. I may be strong, but they will not be. How am I to reconcile myself to my fate, a fate which I have chosen! Better to call it a destiny of mine and my father's making.

You see, Happy's mother was a mother, and she did not have to figure anywhere because she was everywhere. That was why she was excluded from thoughts and conversations. Mothers do not need an advocate. They do not need to be present because they are ever-present.

Happy hit the bottom of heaven. *'What is God? God is just a direction to direct one's happy goals. For the good of humanity, after all, what is one if not humanity? What is love? Love is for yourself. Love is not mucus and membranes. Love is the universe, and taking a cue from a great man, love is by the universe, of the universe, and for the universe! Why restrict it to one or many persons, the girl Money? Life is beyond Money and money, but it cannot survive without money. This is a paradox, How am I to revolt and be free?'*

Happy thought, and at midnight realized he had sunk like a stone to the bottom of life's pool. This was not to be misunderstood. Happy had sunk to a disastrous depth with scotch and women, but to sink to the bottom of life's pool is to understand it completely. He had understood life completely, and would emerge and take a fresh gasp of what probably lay beyond what puny men called life.

Happy lay awake the whole night, caught in shimmering reflections of stars in the sea. Fire and water. He was exactly that — zen. An attraction of opposites, a harmony amidst disharmony. This was life. No constant peace. To find peace in disquiet is the quiet of meditation.

Happy realized at dawn, another dawn, another dawn, that running away from life was not the answer, but that one had to rush into the bull of a life and grab it by its horns. That would be a life completely led. Neither saintly nor monkish, but mannish! Or womanly, considering what the Israeli lady had told him, that, "To be empowered doesn't mean losing one's femininity, doesn't mean enrolling in an army and not wearing a lacy bra, but to be strong when it comes to one's choices in life and to be soft when it comes to one's man!"

Happy wanted his own strong and soft woman after having led a life of disquietude. He was tired and the morning sun would probably shine upon him with both their glory.

Happy slept blissfully and had a delightfully tragic daymare.

He dreamt that he was begging Money to come back to him and she had reluctantly agreed. It was pathetically beautiful. She was coming and going.

Happy was sinking in an infinite hole.

Money would not come to him and he would not be salvaged from the dumps of life.

Happy had sunk and drowned in the depths of love.

Love was nothing according to Money and everything according to Happy.

But they would never again meet across the infinitudes of solitudes.

Money was in all probability happy, but Happy was definitely not happy with money and without Money; soon, with his excesses, he would not be left with any money!

Happy felt suffocated. He desperately missed Money. He had a little money, but was lost without Money.

Happy woke up.

It was a melancholic evening with a melancholic sun.

Happy screamed into the dying sun, "Money!"

And was left without both.

Happy had lost.

All he had was his philosophy.

Love is love lost, if not anything else.

Happy was a fool. He was lost after having understood everything. That is the death of a philosopher. That is what love does to you. It kills you.

Happy suddenly reached for his bottle of scotch and found it empty. He panicked and thought he must be running out of money. He immediately called up his chartered accountant from his laptop, the one he had been using to run his imagery screens with, with which he had managed to monopolize seekers' search for truth on his island. After the call got over, and Happy was assured that he had a considerable sum in his bank account with which to waste his life with, he suddenly, again, understood what he had always understood, that, *'Men are afraid of death, of the death of all they know and have come to love and hate, and therefore make up God and an afterlife of the soul, if not of the mind. That consciousness is just an accident which men come to cherish. That nothing is either of the universe's or ours, but that all is one. We are the bottle of scotch, the scotch, and the drunkards too. Drunk with life we are and are scared to lose whatever it is that we think we lose. The Buddha was right. Only suffering is the truth, and if we do not suffer, we live and do not die.'*

Happy was a broke writer and knew the power of poems. He wrote a poem to Selene at midnight. It was a full moon night. She loved minimalism, and he wanted to reach out to his friend.

He called it, "Life".

Life is
Why ask
No bliss
Arcane task
Death's kiss
This place
In space

Forever
Thereafter
Can be
Paradise see
If only you let go
Of all that you know

The poem was rhyming, and most importantly, symmetric. Happy was happy after again understanding his unsettling understanding, and knew Selene would be too.

For you see, after all, both of them were poets. And poets see life as it is.

Happy had learnt something profound from his buddy Selene. She was the straight and tall arcanut tree of existentialism. Intoxication, yes, but only if you stand proud and stand straight and stand tall. And intoxication only after reaching the top and harvesting the fruit of your labors. He realized how foolish he had been to be caught in two minds when dealing with people. You can either bend of your own free will or stand straight. Being bent by will of others or by your own mindlessness invites only pain. There is no gain to either of the involved parties. However, Happy realized that he had mostly been broken by trying to stand up straight in the face of fate. There was no shame in that. That was life, and his buddy's name was Life who had taught him a better life. Happy felt vindicated by this chain of reasoning which unshackled him from the unreasonableness of life. Happy thought, *'Life is but something to be led without analyzing, for no amount of analyzing is sufficient, and that is the only infinity, not God.'* Life was life, and that was again the death of a philosopher.

It was a glorious morning; as almost all mornings are in

paradise, but this one was especially glorious as with the rising sun Happy made a decision that the next two or three days would be the twilight of his stay on his Island of Monk Evolved. The decision spread like wildfire. In the next few days, boats and boats of devotees started thronging Happy's island ashram. Happy decided to shoot answers to quickfire questions across varied fronts.

"Am I living in the Matrix Happy? You must have seen the movie?"

"Since your brain experiences all your five senses reacting to the world, the world can be replaced by a program within an electronic machine controlling electrical and chemical inputs to yours and others' combined brain, within, and controlled, by the Matrix. But, no, you are not living in the Matrix as of right now. This is real life."

"What is responsible for life, Happy?"

"You must have seen the oscilloscope monitoring a patient's heartbeats in hospitals. Constancy, either of happiness or sadness, is death. At the risk of sounding trite, change is the only constant, and hopefully, originally, responsible for life."

"Is your will to live that of meaning, power, or pleasure, Happy?"

"Perfection of Shoonya, everything and nothing!"

Suddenly a senior monk arrived to pay his respects to the soon-to-be-gone monk Happy.

Happy paid his respects by asking his own questions to which he already knew the answers so that the spectators could benefit from their dialogue.

"The question of questions, O' monk of monks, 'Is living in the moment possible, for if you are cut off from past experiences, how will you deal with the future?'"

"That is why it is called as living in the present moment, young monk, and at that moment, the brain is not thinking, but transcending!"

"Why is the search the misery?"

"Because, monk Happy, understanding from Zhuangzi, the very search for happiness is the cause of unhappiness, yin and yang!"

"Does love exist, old monk?"

"Yes, with hate. Do you think the Taoists were born yesterday? People corrupt love because they are filled with hate. As the young grow old, their love grows old. You are wavering young one. Are you growing old?"

The old monk and the young monk bowed to each other, and the elder left.

A cosmopolitan couple, with glasses of wine in their hands, came in the old monk's stead. They were the yang to his yin.

The woman laughed, "Life is a gift. Why do people throw away gifts?"

Happy took her wine glass, emptied it, and laughed, "Pity them. They aren't used to receiving any. However, I, for one, unlike almost all monks and other people, cherish all gifts of life. I enjoy!"

The man asked a serious question, "Why do people pray to gods with supernatural powers?"

"Because, my dear chap," said Happy taking his wine glass. "They don't want to put in the effort to work upon a plane or a submarine. They want a quick fix. They want to be Superman and Aquaman with the help of a prayer," and emptied the glass in a gulp.

The woman giggled, "What is the addiction of the teetotaler, Happy?"

"Not drinking," smiled Happy, and became serious. "But then again, any addiction is an addiction, and life is the biggest." He smiled again. "Go get drunk on life you two!"

There were some random questions too.

"What is an impossibility?"

"You can't exactly call it an impossibility, but it is easy to believe in God and live and die, but difficult not to and to…"

"True impossibility then?"

"A single general truth for all specimens. Even the best minds cannot find one common truth for a man and a woman. Mankind's woe is the search for that truth."

"Isn't truth the same as beauty and hence same for all?"

"Unfortunately, beauty is also numbers and marketing. Sadly, truth, beauty, can be made a matter of statistics and hence varies erratically."

Happy got up for a break, but a joker demon came shrieking and laughing from a boat and wound up like the Batman's Joker in front of him, begging and bullying him into answering his questions then and there.

Happy was neither horrified nor harassed. He wanted to make the most of his last days on the island and thus permitted joker demon to laugh and cry and rave and rant, "Go ahead JD!"

"How did you arrive at your inanimate philosophy?" shrieked JD.

"By losing all fear."

"How did you lose all fear?" laughed JD.

"By cutting off all whom I loved. If you don't have anyone to love and lose, there is no fear either."

"Why do you live then?" cried JD tearfully.

"Desire. Desire has nothing to do with love, and one needs to live for life's sake."

The rollercoaster of emotions in JD continued while Happy calmly maintained his calm.

"How in hell can you live in peace using your inanimate philosophy?"

"Have you ever seen an unpeaceful wall?"

"What is your desire anyway?"

"To intersect with other walls of Korn in Fields of Gold, idiot! Heard good music from great bands?"

"Happy, you are crazy!"

"The world is a lunatic asylum, JD!"

"So, you feel alive like a lunatic!"

"Yes, for we were dead when we were born."

"You are sicker than me!"

"Is the world healthy, JD?"

"You are shifting the blame for your inanimate philosophy!"

"I am not the earth to shift its tectonic plates and separate!"

"Will you die a peaceful monk, Happy?"

"The most! But then again, I was never born!"

"How does your nonsense help others, Happy?"

"To almost feel no pain, for pain is not so painful, but agony over agony is. You see JD, I really enjoy my visits to my dentists, for they give me the chance to test my philosophy!"

"You have paid the ultimate price for peace, Happy!"

"Yes, love demands sacrifice. To end all thoughts."

Twilight had come and left. The fires were blazing now and scotch was inviting. Happy, who had stopped all thought, got up and went to join his devotees who were eagerly waiting for him to come and join them in the farewell festivities which had begun prematurely.

JD, the joker demon, slinked away into the night sea.

That night, long after midnight, Happy lay awake with the

scotch dead inside him. He had never felt intoxicated beyond sane limits, and today he was as normal as a rock on whose head scotch had been poured. The reason was:

Happy hadn't told his devotees why he was leaving. Many had scoffed at his philosophy. He hadn't minded, for they were right to as philosophy had no place in life, and Happy the philosopher had died long ago. He had only been keeping up appearances to expose the foolishness of monks and philosophies, himself and his in particular. Empty words and their jugglery had no place in a life where the only warmth was from the early morning sunshine during coffee with fathers and mothers and wives and children. He had seen celibate philosophers philosophize about sex. He wanted all, and his own family was one of everything. The death of a philosopher would be truly complete only when he gave life to a child of his own. He had philosophized that a life without God had meaning only in procreation, life's continuation. He would stand by at least this one of his least talked about philosophies. With this turnaround of a monk, in time, his devotees would learn, and unlearn about being his devotees and start to think for themselves. They had seen his love with Babe and Butt, and later they would see his fidelity. They would learn that life was meant to be lived according to society's norms, a society which had evolved from barbarians and whores into husbands and wives with children. He had made a mockery of his life, yin, to see the other side, white, yang, and now that he had seen yin, black, he would become pure and bathe in the waters of matrimony. But would the so-called decent society accept him after all his transgressions and his mockery of it? Would he be able to drown himself in it if they opened up their lake to him, now that he had fallen in love with the sea? Only time would tell.

The energetic Happy fell asleep at dawn and even the afternoon sun couldn't burn his naked body enough to wake him up before twilight. It was only when twilight's pastel colors fell across his smooth body did he wake up to his devotees waiting impatiently around his bedroom of sand.

Happy immediately fell to the task after a quick dip in the soothingly energizing sea.

It would be a discussion of depths beside the sea at dusk.

"Why do you say humanity has no humanity and has fallen to great depths, deep sea Happy?"

"Because of these three levels of truths, O' wise Turt, for the turtle that you are:

1. Men love to hate what they love but can't have.
2. Men treat their equals with scorn because they want to feel superior.
3. Men treat the less equal with hate in fear that they will become their equals."

"Who wins in a torn relationship, O' plumber of depths?"

"When sharks tear up a relationship, the poor fish, which stops obsessing and starts living, survives, O' wise Turt!"

"The ocean, water, the stuff of life, gives peace to the torn pirate heart, O' navigator of storms, Happy."

"Dear Turt, non-attachment to even peace is absolutely necessary to attain the greatest peace. This is life."

Happy knew what he was talking about, for he was on his way towards real life, and not a life of philosophy.

"What are life's needs, O' scavenger of depths, Happy?"

"Turt, nothing is indispensable in life, not even life itself," said the happily-sad Happy.

"How can a relationship between a shark and a dolphin be built, Happy?"

"On common, and not uncommon grounds, O' wise Turt!"

"How can you presume to be always right, O' pirate of seas of thought?"

"How can anyone be more right than one? After all, one is the touchstone!"

"Why can't one get along with another, Happy?"

"Because, another is not one, Turt!"

Happy the symmetrical poet was happy with this reply of his.

Turt continued, "Why do pirates have so many superstitions, Happy?"

"Because, Turt, when death lives next door, you wish for other doors... True of all humans!"

The devotees around the blazing fires broke out into such thunderous applause, that it felt like it would rain the fires dead.

Turt knew that the time to party had come, so the last question was put forth, "What is life's greatest paradox, O' pirate Happy?"

"That it is both costly and cheap, O' wise Turt. Let's party now!"

It was dawn and Happy would leave at sundown. The last few questions and answers would be to the point. Happy was tired. Real life was waiting and to him it seemed unreal. The death of a philosopher would be followed by the burial of philosophy. Maybe, it would burn.

A doctor and engineer couple asked during the time of the virus, "Happy, pray tell what is a true panacea?"

"Turning a disease into a cure, dears."

"Engineers are always right. Computers don't make mistakes!" laughed the happier of the couple.

"Engineers are right for themselves. It doesn't mean they are right for others, who make mistakes!" laughed Happy.

"Doctors don't make mistakes?" was asked by the engineer.

"The human body is a mistake, but perfect, Shoonya!" philosophized the decaying philosopher.

"You say karma is between humans, so what exactly is it?" asked the professionals.

All the while Happy had been playing with his computer, as he had done so many times in the past when he was seated in front of his screens, fielding questions, and playing the visual of his and his questioners' audio onto the screens. He had used pretty graphics that had left his audiences spellbound. He was a performer par compare.

A saint was shown to have asked the question on the left screen.

A cauldron of boiling vegetables appeared on the center screen.

"Dears, it is human vegetables boiling in sin and leaking into each other, nothing else, nothing supernatural," answered Monk on the right screen after the monk Happy.

"Who eats the stew, your God and Devil?" the saint on the screen asked after the professionals on the ground in front of Happy.

"No, how absurd! It is thrown back into the primordial soup of Darwin, Dawkins, and Associates," laughed the monks, as Darwin's image replaced the cauldron on the center screen.

"What drives you Happy?" asked the professionals and Vincent Van Gogh who replaced the saint on the left screen as the center screen turned blank.

Monks laughed, "Gnaw is a greater drive than glad, you know that, Vin!"

All screens turned blank.

"Tell us the greatest thought," was asked by the professionals on the ground and an image of a doctor and an engineer on the left screen.

De-evolving human apes on the right screen answered,

"Don't think.

"On second thought…"

"If you are going to regret the thought later, kill yourself quickly, else the thought will come back to haunt and kill you slowly."

Again, all the screens went blank.

"So, you will die happily with your wisdom, Happy?" asked the professionals in front of Happy and Vin on the left screen facing his Sunflowers and then Monk.

"No, Vin, like you, heartbroken in pain and misery."

Trend on Mend, Tom, the black cat appeared. He reminded Happy of the color of the Ethiopian he had been with. Happy decided that Yin would get to ask some of the last few questions. He started walking towards the Yang lighthouse to pack up along with black Tom at his heels.

"Please educate me. Is there nothing beyond the grave, either above or below?"

"O' Nine Lives Tom, I just see animals, eating to mate and procreate, but unwilling to suffocate."

"But Happy, God, rebirth, and more than nine lives, ensure no crime!"

"Pussy, actually quite the opposite. They ensure war and terrorism. If men realized that they had only one life, they would live it fully and well."

Pussy meowed in pain, "Why do people lie and cheat, Happy?"

Happy had started climbing the stairs of the lighthouse with pussy at his heels, "Survival. It is survival of the degenerate. This is the degenerate truth of evolution."

Tom screeched, "I am chosen to be resurrected, Happy!"

Happy kept quiet until they reached his room at the top of the lighthouse. He then opened a carton of milk and said, "You are the son without a father. The universe has no creator. It always existed, in one form or another, and you too pussy Tom. Drink from life."

He poured the milk into two glasses and began throwing out the bottles of scotch from his treasury. It was time for sobriety.

But pussy was addicted to milk, so Tom asked, "Is life meant to be squandered fully?"

"Of course, yes! Why do you want to leave anything for death to take! Drink fully pussy."

Time had come for silence and finally it came for sunset.

At twilight, when Happy was about to leave his Lighthouse of Beauty on The Island of Monk Evolved surrounded by The Sea of Humanity, two final questions were asked of Happy.

The last two questions among innumerable from his devotees had been chosen arbitrarily as Happy himself believed that everything was nothing but an accident.

Two because, Happy wanted to be part of a couple.

"Why do we smile at others' misfortune?"

"It is our misfortune to be unfortunate."

"Aren't you hurting others by your philosophy Happy?"

"I will never agree to that, for you see, this was my island," said Happy at the moment his second foot was lifted off the beach and into a boat.

Happy was soon gone.

The devotees started worshipping Monk who had climbed to the top of a coconut tree.

All were left alone.

Epilogue

It was night. Happy was between the mainland and the island. He was no longer confused as to which was life and which was death. He was heading towards life, the mainland, for it had been the burial of a philosopher on the island. Philosophy had been cremated, but its smoldering embers still tried to fly over the sea with him towards life.

Happy knew that one cannot be alone on an island for life, that life called for a simple, no-philosophy, relationships-filled existence on the mainland of life. Death was waiting on the mainland too, but he would not die alone, and life asked for theism, God, to help people live and die peacefully. His philosophy had been perfectly right, but it helped nobody. "Of what use is a philosophy which cannot provide solace to men during life and asks them to die a purposeless death after which is nothing?" cried Happy standing up in the boat and rocking it. The boatman stopped the boat and smiled, for he had seen disbelievers like Happy giving up their philosophy after it had burnt their senses.

Happy saw the boatman's smile in the night and felt he must interpolate within and extrapolate. He knew the boatman had ferried innumerable devotees between his island and the mainland, and was wise to his arcane, abstruse philosophy. So, he began a reverse Siddhartha on Vasudeva, a philosophy which he had kept hidden, even from himself, for he knew that only mouths and ears, and that too only when in sync, produced the best philosophy instantaneously, "Life is an unseen energy. To experience it, you must live life fully. Open your mind, and most importantly, your heart, for what is life except love? If you don't love the ones who hate you, you haven't truly loved. I loved Money, indecipherably, but it is time to let go of her if I have to love the whole universe, and anyway, she is a part of it. I want to stand outside the universe and love it as my child. I want to be God, but can I?"

Stars sparkled over the boat that was gently bobbing on the waves.

Happy messaged these thoughts and more to Selene as he continued speaking aloud, "My thoughts are scattering like the pieces of my life. Please amalgamate them into a masterpiece stained-glass window which will let in sunrays into the church of humanity."

"Selene, I realize it now. We have to understand Shoonya, Circle. Truth is that the past is the future and vice versa. Eternal Recurrence. I have been right!

"This is rebirth. This is God. This is Hindu philosophy combined with the German one; however, to combine the Evolution of science with the Kaal Chakra, I have minted a new currency for philosophy stamping it with the die of science. There are infinite alternate Big Bangs, births, and Big Crunches, deaths, of the universe. Each time there is a new and different evolution. Time moves in a circle, and each time evolution takes place!

"There is no single truth. Science has one and others another."

The full moon shone and Happy became happy.

He whispered, "Dear Selene, how stupid I have been to wander and not gather! I found you as a result of my wanderings. Please tell me I am not misled by wanderlust...

"The circular Yin and Yang symbol, why Yin? Because it is conflict that keeps us alive. Friction is energy.

"If the unknown were known, we wouldn't strive to know, and rot.

"I never prayed when I stood in front of God, but my mind was always a placid pool. My struggle to understand is mine and mine alone, hidden deep within. I am an underwater volcano. I live to unmask the mystery of being. I will strive, and struggle is what we should all desire.

"I am confused. People tell me that they do not see bad in me. Is it my father's money that makes me good or am I inherently good? I will have to become a beggar to understand, but then again, aren't we all beggars, praying for rescue from our fate, Selene?"

The boat started moving, and soon, as quickly as life meets death, Happy's boat from the island of death, met the mainland of life.

Happy jumped out of the boat, and climbed a tall, straight, and proud coconut tree of existentialism upon the beach, and he, the evolved monk, howled like his capuchin monkey, Monk, for a mate, for the naked ape had arrived.

By Selene

If the world is an ocean vast
We're its ephemeral waves
Rising up for a moment fleeting
Then vanishing away

These numbered days we have
Why paint them with sorrow
When in our hands we have
To sculpt a happier tomorrow

We might not have answers
To all questions that life flings
But let that not deter us
From spreading our wings

Let's learn to spell life as L O V E
Fill forlorn hearts with hope
To those be compassionate
Who're walking on tightropes

No one can ever perceive
What lies beyond Death
So let's make the most of life
With each drawn breath

How Happy Screwed Up After He Went Back
He wrote poems

1

Bidar Poetry

A melody wafts my way
I blow it away
Why, pray?

2

A poem for myself:

It is today again
I am alone again
Nothing will change again

3

They cheat you
They stab you
But they can't take you
Away from you
And this poem is for you

4

Selene…

My friend is an enigma
I the world's stigma
But the charisma
Lies in our Karma

5

Karma

Someone asked
Are you working
In my glow I basked
Myself I am satisfying
Sorry that you asked
You don't know being

6

Fly

I am but a buffoon
In love with a balloon
Trying to grasp its string
To experience flying
But my weight is such
That of the world it carries much
Myself I need to let go
If into the skies I have to flow

7

Love or something like it

People's love is arranged
Mine happened
Which is more powerful
Is left to the tasteful

8

Kafka's The Trial

I tried
At my effort
Life sighed
And said braveheart

At the end of trial of lover
I realized
Judge, jury, and executioner
Had been yours truly beloved

9

Philosopher's Dilemma

You say Philosophy
I say mon ami
Need money

You ask why
And I cry
No Philosophy on stomach empty

10

Dad's

Please give me time
Please give me life
Just for one year of mine
Lot you have suffered
Lot you have endured
Need your love now
More when I am too old my love
At least let me feel
You care and love me for real
Please tolerate one more
Year for life to take shape once more
If it is suffering
I will all better things to you bring
Before I let go
I want one more year full of peace and love
This is my last request
To a baby put by the gods in my basket

11

The Secret

Secret to joy
Lies in knowing my boy
That not only ends sadness
But so also does happiness

Life is ended
By death fated
And this truth my son
Will live as long as the sun

But you shouldn't die
Every moment
But life live
As if it were your last moment

Then you will be fearless
Truly deathless
Traveling towards immortality
Through the portal of mortality

12

Twins

It takes a mountain
To shoulder another twin

If two minds match
They can withstand a thousand

Why seek a crowd
When our unified minds can be by the very gods loved

13

Liberty

Love is a statue worshipped
But seldom accomplished

Fallen may be the man
For the woman

Fails to realize he
That life surpasses he & she

So also her
In her fervor

Emotions are but stupid solutions
To life's conundrums

Rise to be
What you can be

14

Afternoon Blues

A life simple
Is what I would consider ample
To bring a dimple
Upon my cheek with its stubble

15

Bidar

Bidar with its mosques and tombs
Gurudwaras and temples with gods from many wombs
Has swallowed the atheist me
And transformed into an anti- atheist me

Pray what is the difference
You may ask in your innocence
I reply the love of people
For whom God is a need my love

Let me not take away
A need which can sway
Death into another life's way
And who am I anyway

16

Ode to Professor Shivaprasad

Prasad
Was the immortal's prasad

To the hungry
Both in minds and stomachs empty

Poetry
Was fed and education given to all and sundry

By him who would not be
Let by his son bygone be

I cried at the tribute
To the immortal by his son astute

And wished one day
I too could in the same manner over my father's death hold
sway

17

Struggle

The misery of life
Lies in being
Yourself in its strife
And unbecoming

Emperor don't kill
Others with ill will
But yourself subjugate
And throne abdicate

For you have
Only yourself to rule
Be brave
Find in yourself your fuel

18

Equal

Nothing superior
To feel about
The inferior
Is not

The autorickshaw driver
Is your brother
The sweeper
Your sister

Let not money
Blind you buddy
For if it does
Your soul goes

Think and act
Not act and think
Otherwise you will sink
During life's final act

19

Release

When of anything there is excess
Builds up stress
You obsess
And of life is less

That thing senseless
Release
Mind torture cease
And be free of duress

Fly
Be a whimsical butterfly
With false weight shed
No more tears will be shed

20

What is love?

Greatest love unspoken
Not between man and woman
But with child
Love subtly wild

Witnessed it today
Between brother and his daughter
Reminded me of yesterday
Me with my father

21

Self-actualization

If life were to be
What we wished it to be

Where would be the fun
And challenges begun

Reach for the impossible
Actualize the improbable

22

Truth

Nobody can determine your happiness
Fear is desire
Desire is fear
In life be mindless

For no mind
Is truly kind
Accept
Reject

Neti neti
Is advocated by the negative
Through this entreaty
Reach the positive

23

Giving

When you are giving
You are favouring
But yourself
And no other's self

Give
Yourself forgive
Live
Anew

Liberate
Don't suffocate
Create
Like minds amalgamate

24

Politics

Politics' mastery
Is not achieved without slavery

A politician
Is but a suave barbarian

Self rule
Should be the rule

25

Poor

When I see the poor
And am unable to help them be
Of poverty free
I realize I myself am poor

Of what use is my degree
Language and sophistication
If knowledge cannot change a situation
It is death's decree

26

Important

It's not important
Who you know is important

Neither does it matter
Whether you matter

Be a Shoonya
Ekalavya

Everybody matters
None are masters

27

Apology of a writer

I tried
I lived

But upon
The mercy of others begotten

Truth I may have spoken
But mostly by others forsaken

For what is life
But strife

I assure you all
That the fall

Of Adam and Eve
Will come when you will this writer not forgive

28

Crowd

Today lost myself in the crowd
For I am the crowd

I am the press
I am the easily swayed class

I am the rich bugger
I am the pauper beggar

I am the influencer
I am the influenced sinner

But who am I father
Just water

Flow
Be by algae aglow

River
And stagnant water

I will evaporate
Of that much I am sure

29

Dad's

Son
Get up with the dawn sun
Let us get going
Journey has begun my darling
Long way to go
Time is limited this you know
Destiny is calling us
And we will make it without fuss
For we are driven by
Our combined Spirit my boy
We are driven by mutual love soaring
So let us get going

30

Dad's

Life is to live
Not to cry over spilt milk please believe
Nor to mourn over many a past mishap
For the present and future are ours old chap
Past is erased
Of no consequence the dead
Live in the moment
Peace and serenity invent
For others
And they will be your powers
You will spread joy and happiness
Bliss will be yours my son in oneness

31

Epiphany

A writer irresponsible
Is to his readers unfaithful

How many can understand
His stand

Like actors who played
Batman's Joker prayed

For sanity in ordinary life
But succumbed to the mad character's strife

He too has to be a mad scotch swigging philosopher
To sink into character

And that created the book
Death of a Philosopher with Raj's guts hanging by a hook

And this trauma is being responsible
And to his readers faithful

32

Parents

How can a child be happy
If it makes its parents sad
It is bound to be unhappy
No matter what it does to make itself glad

Its actions
Are reactions
Upon its parents' happiness
And sadness

Awake child slumbering
Stop encumbering
Understand being
And yourself forgiving

For once you forgive
Yourself and others that bent you
Will you stand up straight
And make things right

33

Dad's

My Life

A tiny wave in a universal sea
Trying to reach the shore is me
Sometimes part of calm
Sometimes of storm
Once in a while of tsunami angrily born
But always moving on
Trying to retain identity
Forging relationships mighty
Creating emotions and love almighty
As shore nears my friend
Realize the temporariness and end
Of all that was once the trend
Into what will parts of me transform
Cannot console those many a new name and form
With the philosophy of let go and be reborn
What and whom
I feel part of a whole never died or born
Need my wife and son
To hold my hands and lead me on
To the shore so that I can move on
I desire peace, love and serenity

Confused with uncertainty
God, take my consciousness
And put me to the deep sleep of bliss
For eternity

—Tormented Father of a loving Son Raj and Husband of a caring Wife.
LOVE ALL. & Eternally Grateful to All…

34

Corruption

To be uncorrupted
In a society corrupted

Not to yell
When they untruths yell

Maintaining calm
In the face of an illogical storm

Requires self-effacement
And being within content

Is it hard
Asked the bard

And himself answered
Impossible if you don't life itself discard

35

Khan

We the hungry
We the angry
Angry because we are Tengri
Lord of lightning for all and sundry
Enthusing the greatest Mongol Genghis
That the world is his
Can't we kiss
And live in bliss

36

Dad's

Good Day

To be joyous is intrinsic
Flowers bloom, birds make music
Sun shines, zephyr blows cool and fragrant
Can we not be happy for a moment
If so, we can be for a minute, hour, day
Over whole life hold sway
Create joy, happiness, love
Spread, share and experience bliss my love
Maybe we have come into existence
Not to mess up things around us without sense
But to live and love
Care and serve

37

Actor

You don't want to do
But show what you can do

You don't want to live for a cause
But applause

You sit in a silent club
You sit in a crowded pub

And raise your voice
To your importance emphasize

Be free
Of even yourself to see

You don't need anyone
That you are already someone

If others don't
Don't make them pleasing your wont

Then fly
Away from the crowd you whimsical butterfly

Flowers are waiting
Your nectar they are seeking

38

Dad's

Reality Unraveled

Life nucleated
Born amalgamated
Living began
Full of desire, ego and fear over and over again
Felt empty having everything
Inner me desired a sublime something
Peace, serenity and bliss
Given with a soft kiss
Time was passing
Inner me craved the blessing
Of answers eluding man
Who, what and why I am
Yesterday, I had a dream
Life appeared as illusion's scream
Started floating and drifting
Lost sense of time and being
Space appeared infinite
Realized I am just the tiniest speck finite
Drifted through universes
All were expanding like my lost senses
Specks like me everywhere

Kept on drifting through universes somewhere
Sudden realization occurred
I am the cosmos blurred
Integral part of the cosmos' soul
Part of the whole
Family, friends and all
With the cosmos well integrated
I with my loved ones celebrated
Through the cosmos is the journey of life
This reality dawned upon me without any strife
Felt peace, serenity and bliss
Why create mess and fuss which are everywhere amiss
Felt let me not be unhappy
And continued my journey through the cosmos feeling happy

39

Nama and Rupa

If I my name remove
I will be left with form
If form I then remove
I will be left only with love's storm

40

Dad's

Nature Awakens

It is dawn
Life becomes lively without a single yawn
Sun begins to shine
Birds sing songs sublime
Flowers bloom
Wind blows away gloom
Animal and plant world comes to life
Whole ecosystem gets activated with strife
But all contribute towards a healthy system where we die
To stay alive
Let us get up
And get going with chin up
Enjoy nature's celebration
Contribute our share to an amalgamated situation
Make the day a celebration
And create on Earth's station
Heaven amidst the multiverse's many a station
Let coexistence
Or no existence
Be our mantra of sense
Realize all have a purpose

Beauty, joy and peace
Love will prevail
Bliss will be ours in the tale
Which eternity will tell

41

Dad's

Love You

I love you in bliss
I tell you this
For me love is
To share joy which is never amiss
To care and share
To feel as one always aware
To be one in sorrow
To feel you as my responsibility today and tomorrow
To create a lively life together
To love what you love forever
To be part of your happiness my lover
Love means you are me brighter
Love is to part never

42

Fraud

How many excuses
How many lies

Will you give
And tell yourself man alive

Are you seeking
What others you are telling

Or are you sure
Of the you pure

Become naked
Then will you be sacred

43

Futility

If you think
You can get empathy
You wrongly think
For there is not even sympathy

Why cry
And die
Wanting from someone
When you have to die alone

44

Ode to Twin

You keep on writing ahead
With that someone in your head

Who you hope and know
Will understand your pen's flow

Such a friend among six billion others
Is enough to land you among flowers

Do not pick from that bed
To make a wreath for the dead

But let the fragrance of your art
Embellish the garden's heart

45

V Day

On this Valentine's Day
I decided it would no more be self-Vengeance Day

I have decided to love myself so much
That nothing outside of me can touch

Clean
Will be now my sunbeam

46

Dad's

Change and Chance

Son you are growing younger
I am growing older
Paradox of a sufferer
Seen us grow in directions different
Both conditioned different
Embedded with values different
Matter of change and chance
But invisible bond still exists in permanence
Appears like care and concern
Love, joy and pain still exist my son
Life is evolving
Meanings are changing
Everything seems to be a dance of atoms
Life of illusions
Appears only to be change of forms
What are all these struggles
Have we control over the battles
Change, chance and our desires
Life appears to be
A complicated and complex existential tree
Mixture of basic entities of cosmos

Where we are nothing what we think and see
Let us drift and not resist
Sail smoothly through the cosmos to exist
Son, we are aliens to each other
There is need for living in harmony of the old and newer
Let us enjoy the show of the creator

47

Idiocy

Narcissus
Is all of us
Staring at death
Imagining rebirth

48

Moment

Time
Doesn't exist I blaspheme

Neither
Does space I beg to differ

In your tiny mind
To reality you are blind

In the ecstasy of Shoonya
Space and time are ya

49

Truth

If there was no shoulder
To place upon your woe boulder
Would you climb up the mountain to your agony emboss
You Sisyphus

50

Life

Why cry
When there is none to sigh
Upon your sadness
Which they will never understand in their madness

51

Basic

No such thing as love emotion
But only facilitation
For procreation

For you are but atoms
Whose beginnings are buried below fathoms
With unclear destinations

Live
Celebrate
Forget

52

Dad's

Life is Simple

Simple is true
Simple is beautiful
Simple is spiritual
Happy life is simple should be your cue

Birds sing melodiously
Flowers bloom beautifully
Butterflies glide smoothly
Nature evolves effortlessly

Why humans make fuss
Make life a mess
Why life is analyzed
Why not simply lived

Why complicate life
Why make it a complex strife
Why need a creator
Why need a soul sister
Why talk of consciousness
Why of after-life bliss

Or of a new life's kiss

Let people be flowers
Let them be birds
Let them be plants
Let them be whimsical butterflies

Let simple people be simple
Let us not create illusions ample
Let them be more human
Let them know my son
Simple is the seal of true upon the sun
Let them glide through
The cosmos like whimsical butterflies true

Naturally lived a life
Is a fulfilled life
Why worry about death
Why of destiny after last breath

53

Anti — Atheist

Atheist you
If you
Want to eradicate God fallacy and religion
What will you give in return

54

Change

Son of an unhappy king
Is a happy prince
Till time comes for him to be king

Abdicate
Or to become subjugate
Becomes obfuscate

55

Day and Night

When I woke
I thought the fire of life I would stoke

But as the hot noon fell
Felt caught up in anger's swell

Wasted day till evening
When I saw my dark side emerging

At twilight
I felt myself light

And as the dark descended
I ascended

For in the nadirs
Dwell zeniths of your tears

Where you shine bright
In the world's night

56

Troy

Achilles
Was not born to success

Knew he would die
If he fought against love's lie

His mother
Had asked him to reconsider

But immortality
Could not be kept at bay

Achilles fought
A suicide attempt with success fraught

Died he did
But eternity vanquished

57

Way

If you can't boy
In the process take joy

How will you know which station
Is your destination

But alas
The truth is you dumbass

That life is but an indefinite
Self-actualization infinite

58

Why

I was born naked
And none for my permission had asked

They paraded me in society naked
As if for that very purpose they had been tasked

In the noon sun I cried naked
And none for my baked back cared

Finally when the time came for them to me crucify
Each had a nail in their hand to my wrongs rectify

59

Formula 1

I wasn't looking for Twitter popularity
But only for a friend who would have empathy
And found a twin
Yes, I win

60

Dear Elder Brother Crash

They did what they felt justified
Derided
And crucified
Knowing not truth was victimized

In a long tale told short
They were left searching
For their very being
In the true being's life cut short

61

Raw

I strive for flesh
For I was born of two

I stink of lust
For humanity to survive it is must

So why are you arguing
And truth forsaking

That in your loins
Lies future's coins

62

Time

Life is passing by
And I shouldn't be shy

To explore the forbidden
To feel myself forgiven

By life which has so much to offer
And with which I should never differ

Society will scream
But I will not kill my dream

Of having tried to taste
What otherwise would have gone to waste

63

Disidentification

Am
I what I believe I am

Or something better-off
Or worse-off

If I don't know who is me
How can I trust others to judge me

I don't want to be a part of life's jigsaw puzzle
But to be the puzzle

Never trying to know myself
But only to live without self

Never to be a part
But the whole which seeks to depart

From identification
And be a Shoonya sensation

Shoonya which is everything
And nothing

64

Question

Are we alive
Or a dead slave

To whom do we ascribe our life
Succumbing to death's knife

Can't we be liberated
An eagle's power over clouds stated

Fly
Never impersonify

Die
Without having been a lie

65

Cursed

Right knowledge is not just strengthening
But also to the enlightened debilitating

For they do not know
Whether to share it in the now

Or drink its poison
To make many a stupid generation

66

Desire

Why should I desire anything
Since mine is nothing

But then why shouldn't I
For a beggar am I

67

Cobra

I remember the time
When a cobra was held by its throat by a hand of mine

Agreed it was a juvenile
And not grown to full length serpentile

But poison
It was bound to jettison

I tried to throw it away
But clasping my hand by its tail it over my head held sway

I was not afraid
For I had realized that life was a poisonous cobra which said

You may not be afraid
But you can't get rid of me even if you all death houses raid

68

Sadness

You love someone
But you can't become one

For the vicissitudes of life
Have parted you both from life

Why
I cry

And am responded to by a damned society
That you are not fit to be part of our sobriety

But I am drunk
And therefore sunk

In the infinite possibilities
Of there being no fragilities

In man and woman's being
Where they are joined and are a single being

So burn me at the stake
With her as stake

And watching the fire spread
Be in dread

69

Empty

Empty
Seems to be my duty

Where nothing
Is filled with everything

What do you want
And what do you get

When there is nothing to want
And nothing to get

For all is lost
The moment you get and become desire's ghost

70

Freedom

Freedom lies
Not in intoxicants' lies

Nor in your fundamental beliefs
And definitely not in your relationships

But in thinking free
Being even from wisdom free

71

Free

Free
Is what you ought to be

Irrespective
Of what helps you live

If otherwise you suffer
Remember

You are a living slave
Not a dead brave

72

Sixth

Born on the sixth
With a sense sixth

My friend
Knows whom to befriend

Thankfully I am one of the few
To be the lucky new

On this day I remembered
How she had my will strengthened

When on my birthday
I was moping away

So with this poem
I wish to brighten her occasion

Hoping like wild rivers to the sea
Our poems keep twisting of earth's shackles free

And finally evaporating from the oceans without a sigh
Find their way back as new poems to mountains high

73

Dad's

Dear existence
You put me on this earth because of your benevolence
Through the process of birth supposed to make sense
I thought I was somebody
And loved by everybody

Today wisdom has dawned
I have realized after truth has spawned
That I am nobody
Don't belong to anybody
And also energized
That my utility is destroyed

I must return to no man's land
No more search for any bond
Drift as an atom in the cosmos
Free of heartbreaks and pains

74

Dad's

Dear son
Why worry and burn like the sun
Deeply bury
The dead past gory
Don't make hurry
You are not born to worry
Solitude is your might
Cosmos is your action space of delight
Forget time and no need to keep pace
You are a writer with a strong base
An established creator
A thought warrior
Peace, serenity, and bliss you are
God, religion, and spirituality laid bare
Become joy itself
Be happy and make happy without self

75

Love

If time was a tangible watch
It I would break
And free break
But intangible is time
So also space
What you can't see
Cannot be
God similarly
But here I am
Me
The multiverse you want to see and be
I am the vast ocean
In which raging rivers calm down
I am not the rocks
Upon which surf breaks up
Be not a part of me
But me
Who is you
The one existence in eternity

76

Play

All men are kids
Want to play
Play God

Forgive them Father
They know not
That they sin

Child can be forgiven
But not man
For such an irrational transgression

Grow up son
Love your fellow man
And never domination

77

Tragedy in Three

Such a tragic state of humankind
None listen, think, talk, and act
With a directing rational mind

Haunted by self-borne hounds of fear, prejudice, and anger
Inflict wounds on self and another
Hunting and hunted with the help of dogs without a single tear

Men everyday die
When they are meant to live
Fie

If they ask me what have you accomplished
That you feel you can preach
I will simply say I have fully lived

Gale

Not in storm to live
But in its eye

Requires
Sophistication

Not of humankind
But of elements kind

I am but a speck of vapour
Caught in a gale of disaster

But I will rain down in all my fury
And grow roses in deserts of infamy

79

Reena, a Poem

Lotus of love
Black like a charming winter night above

Her eyes twinkle
Stars they sparkle

Like the jewel
Under her soft lips at which I marvel

Her hair like chains
Of anchors

Fasten my ship
To her sea bed

And then I drown
To depths of heaven

80

Wish

I wish
I could

But what
Should be should

Can I
Yes says I

But unfortunately
It takes an eye for an eye

To realize
The non-sublime

Therefore I depart
From the commoner's art

And paint
Van Gogh's Sunflowers impressionist art

Finding in him mania
And also in Kurt Cobain's Nirvana

Our gang of three
Which from society and life is free

Bipolar disorders all
We Three Musketeers our misfortunes recall

And yell
All for one and one for all

And in a war against fools gamely dying
Bring art into being

81

Strength

Why do we bow
To something we do not know

Why not to us
Alexander who tamed Bucephalus

Or Achilles the warrior
Who died knowing his name would last forever

But these men were of a different coin
Which in the ordinary world men don't join

They loved and fought
Without discrimination of either sex or foe

Set an example
For new age warriors whose staple

Should be freedom
Or else annihilation

82

On my epitaph

Is stupid thinking
For there will not be any
For I am the element
Which cannot pertain to either the past, future, or present
And the reason this high flier
Bombards you with his poems which scream dire
Is because he wants you all to know
That you are all not in the truth to know
And I will be lost and found
In this multiverse sound
Only if you all discard the supernatural
And find in me the sexual natural

83

Caress

Sitting in my dark empty room
On a chair in front of windows blocking doom

Shattered is my gloom
When the breeze outside causes satin curtains to swoon

And caress me like a boon
From you know whom

84

Told to asswipes

Your problem is:
I don't want anything
My strength is:
I don't want anything
Either way I win

Blurb

Philosophy
Cannot be
On a stomach empty
Life, love, and philosophy
Form an unholy trinity
All cannot exist in harmony
The holy
Who cry celibacy
Know not what a woman can be
And above all is money

Books by the Author

1. Whimsical Dice (Olympia Publishers, London, 2021)
2. Predator & Prey (Leadstart Publishing Pvt. Ltd., Mumbai, 2021)
3. Rivers (Writers Workshop, Kolkata, 2021)
4. Demystifying God, Eros and Bacchus (Olympia Publishers, London, 2020)
5. Life Unshackled — From Darkness to Light (Leadstart Publishing Pvt. Ltd., Mumbai, 2020)
6. Approaching Death (Writers Workshop, Kolkata, 2019)
7. A Mariachi & A Philosopher On Wheels — A Poem (Leadstart Publishing Pvt. Ltd., Mumbai, 2019)
8. A Writer's Zen (Leadstart Publishing Pvt. Ltd., Mumbai, 2018)
9. Selene — A Poem (Leadstart Publishing Pvt. Ltd., Mumbai, 2017)
10. Poems For Us (Leadstart Publishing Pvt. Ltd., Mumbai, 2017)
11. Poems To Myself (Leadstart Publishing Pvt. Ltd., Mumbai, 2017)
12. Alternative Haikus (Leadstart Publishing Pvt. Ltd., Mumbai, 2017)
13. Buddha In A Mercedes (Leadstart Publishing Pvt. Ltd., Mumbai, 2017)
14. Politics — A love Story (Leadstart Publishing Pvt. Ltd., Mumbai, 2016)

15. Bhakti Sans Religion — Dilemmas in the Search of One's True Inner Self (Leadstart Publishing Pvt. Ltd., Mumbai, 2016)
16. Star Ride to Nirvana (Leadstart Publishing Pvt. Ltd., Mumbai, 2015)
17. Dams across the Flow (Writers Workshop, Kolkata, 2015)
18. Victims Incorporated — Circles of Sub-consciousness (Current Publications, Agra, 2013)
19. What Happened to My Creativity (CreateSpace, USA, 2013)
20. Operation Epiphany — God's Journey on Earth (Writers Workshop, Kolkata, 2012)
21. The Holy Plumber and Other Stories (Writers Workshop, Kolkata, 2009)
22. Abstractions (Writers Workshop, Kolkata, 2007) (with digital art)